Perilous Rivalry

When Siblings Become Abusive

by

Vernon R. Wiehe

with

Teresa Herring

Lexington Books

D.C. Heath and Company · Lexington, Massachusetts · Toronto

Library of Congress Cataloging-in-Publication Data

Wiehe, Vernon R.
Perilous rivalry: when siblings become abusive / Vernon R. Wiehe
with Teresa Herring.
p.   cm.
Includes index.
ISBN 0-669-25006-6 (alk. paper)
1. Adult child abuse victims.   2. Adult child sexual abuse
victims.   3. Incest victims.   4. Brothers and sisters—Crimes
against.   I. Herring, Teresa.   II. Title.
HV715.W493   1991   362.7'6—dc20   90-21845
                                                        CIP

Published simultaneously in Canada
Printed in the United States of America
International Standard Book Number: 0-669-25006-6
Library of Congress Catalog Card Number: 90-21845

The paper used in this publication meets
the minimum requirements of American National Standard
for Information Sciences—Permanence of Paper
for Printed Library Materials, ANSI Z39.48-1984.

Year and number of this printing:

92 93 94 8 7 6 5 4 3 2

This book is dedicated to those adults whose childhoods
were nightmares because of the physical, emotional,
or sexual abuse they experienced from a sibling or siblings.

Contents

Acknowledgments ix

1 An Undetected Problem   *1*

2 Physical Abuse   *7*

3 Emotional Abuse   *24*

4 Sexual Abuse   *45*

5 Parents React to Sibling Abuse   *67*

6 Understanding Sibling Abuse   *84*

7 Lasting Effects   *96*

8 The Difference between Normal and
       Abusive Behavior   *116*

9 Preventing Sibling Abuse   *125*

10 A Final Word   *139*

Bibliography   142
Index   149
About the Authors   153

Acknowledgments

I would like to express my appreciation to the more than 150 survivors of sibling abuse who responded to the research questionnaire which forms the basis for this book. It is my deepest hope that the sharing of these painful childhood memories will result in a greater understanding of sibling abuse by parents and by professionals who work in the field of family violence. This awareness, in turn, may save others from the terror of an abusive sibling.

The following individuals also have my thanks: Dr. David Royce, a friend and colleague who provided encouragement, editing advice, and feedback; Dean Zafar Hasan, for providing a climate of scholarship and publication in the College of Social Work at the University of Kentucky. My deepest appreciation to my wife, Donna, for her love, support, and encouragement.

Vernon R. Wiehe, Ph.D.
Lexington, Kentucky

In addition to the survivors, who have my unending respect, I would like to thank some of those closer to home. David, as always, and Susan, for this book in particular, have my love and appreciation.

Teresa Herring
Silver Spring, Maryland

An Undetected Problem

The following passages are not taken from a script or a novel. They are the statements of adults who, as children, suffered from the nightmare of a still largely undetected form of abuse—*sibling abuse,* or the physical, emotional, and sexual abuse of one sibling by another.

I was raped when I was thirteen years of age—not by a stranger in a dark alley but by my own brother in my own home when he was baby-sitting me and my younger siblings. He threatened to kill me and make it look like an accident if I ever told my parents. I didn't tell, and he used me sexually from then on whenever he wanted.

I would tell my parents how my brother would hit me. "You must have done something to deserve it," they would say. I didn't do anything. He constantly was beating me. If I tried to protect myself or hit him in return, it was proof to them I deserved it. I spent a lot of time hiding from him in order to protect myself.

Recently I was with a group of friends and we were telling about nicknames we had as children. I said I didn't have any nicknames, but all the while we were laughing and talking, the name I was called by my sister kept going around in my head—"lardass." I wouldn't tell them that is how I was known in my house to my sister when I was a child. My parents used to laugh about it. I wasn't laughing; I was crying. My childhood was a nightmare. I don't even want to look at pictures of when I was a child. I threw my school pictures away. The memories hurt so much. At the age of forty-two I have finally found the courage to seek counseling. Maybe I can come out of my shell and enjoy the remaining years of my life.

In order to recognize, prevent, or treat this form of abuse, it is important to understand why it has remained hidden. Sibling abuse is almost certainly not a new problem, and there is evidence that it may be frighteningly widespread. However, in the past it often has been excused, obscured, and dealt with in many inappropriate ways. Some parents have looked the other way, ignored the problem, or simply not believed the pleas of their children. Others have blamed their offspring for prompting—or deserving—such abuse. Still others have labored under the false belief that it is normal behavior and that all kids do it.

One reason behind these misguided responses is that sibling abuse is often confused with sibling rivalry. Parents and even mental health professionals have excused abusive behavior with statements like

"Kids will be kids."

"All kids call each other names"

"Didn't you ever play doctor when you were a kid?"

"It's just normal sibling rivalry."

One or more of these clichés have probably been used in every family with more than one child. They may even be accurate as responses to certain behaviors. But they are inappropriate when applied to the physical, emotional, and sexual *abuse* of one sibling by another. Calling sibling abuse nothing more than sibling rivalry is like labeling physical abuse nothing more than a little discipline. In order to clear up this confusion, it is important to explore the phrase *sibling abuse,* and distinguish it from sibling rivalry.

Sibling abuse, as described by its survivors in the pages that follow, is not typical, not normal, and certainly not deserved—by them or by any other living beings. In addition, their stories clearly show how ignoring the problem, pretending it doesn't exist, believing it will solve itself, or blaming the victim only makes matters worse. The 150 adults who tell their stories here are living testimony both to the horror of sibling abuse and to the terrible effects of parental ignorance, disbelief, and inaction.

Sadly, the impact of sibling abuse on the victim is not over when either the victim or the abuser leaves the home. There are long-term effects to such behavior, and they are also explored in this book. The fear, low self-esteem, anger, and distrust felt by its survivors are only some of its lingering symptoms; drug and alcohol abuse and serious sexual problems are among its other legacies.

History of a Secret

Historically, events occurring behind the closed doors of people's homes have always been private, a family matter. Americans value their rights and freedoms highly, including their right to privacy, and their freedom to behave in their own homes as they see fit. Congress, the courts, police, community, and social service agencies have been reluctant to get involved in anything happening beyond that threshold of the front door.

But this philosophy has recently been challenged—and rightly so—by individuals who have been violated in their own homes: women who have been battered by their husbands; children who have been abused by their parents. Concerned professionals, victims, and the media have worked together to inform the public about these problems. Over time, the physical effects of abuse—including malnutrition, assault, rape, and death—have been recognized as being more than family concerns. Gradually, social agencies have intervened, as the limits of parental and spousal authority have been recognized. The privacy of the home is now open to the scrutiny of the court and allied agencies when the abuse of a family member is suspected. Legislation has been passed to protect the rights of those who cannot defend themselves; and resources have been developed at the state and national levels to prevent and treat child and spouse abuse.

Over the past several decades, this same process of exposing family secrets has also revealed problems such as elder abuse. Along with child and spouse abuse, it, too, has been brought out into the open. These previously private matters have become known and understood; and considerable progress has been made in their detection, treatment, and prevention. But sibling abuse remains closeted; its symptoms go unrecognized, and its terrible effects continue to be ignored.

Sibling abuse must be brought out into the open. Unmasking it is the first step to remedying it. Child abuse was recognized some forty years ago; it existed before that time but was not identified as abuse.

Only through the process of recognition could steps be taken against it. In 1962, an article titled "The Battered Child Syndrome" was published by Dr. C. Henry Kempe and his colleagues at the University of Colorado Medical Center. The article had a tremendous impact in the field of domestic violence and, among other things, coined the phrase *battered child syndrome* as a clinical condition to describe the fractures, burns, wounds, and bruises seen in young victims of physical abuse.

Social historian John Demos explained in his book *Past, Present and Personal* the long-term importance of the article in this way:

> Child abuse evoked an immediate and complex mix of emotions: horror, shame, fascination, disgust. Dr. Kempe and his co-authors noted that physicians themselves experienced "great difficulty . . . in believing that parents could have attacked their children" and often attempted "to obliterate such suspicions from their minds, even in the face of obvious circumstantial evidence." In a sense the problem had long been consigned to a netherworld of things felt but not seen, known but not acknowledged. The "Battered Child" essay was like a shroud torn suddenly aside. Onlookers reacted with shock, but also perhaps with a kind of relief. The horror was in the open now, and it would not easily be shut up again.

A similar shroud must now be torn aside on the physical, emotional, and sexual abuse of one sibling by another.

Purpose and Scope of This Book

The purpose of this book is to bring sibling abuse out into the open where it can be recognized and dealt with as a serious problem. To start that process, some survivors of sibling abuse have volunteered to explain how it happened, how their parents reacted to it, what effect it has had on their lives, and what could have been done to prevent it.

In order to locate survivors who were willing to speak out, a research questionnaire on sibling abuse was advertised in several major newspapers, and in professional association newsletters. In addition, notices were sent to organizations working in the field of family violence. These ads and notices asked people who had been physically, emotionally, or sexually abused by a sibling when they were growing up to write away for a questionnaire, to which they could respond anonymously. No fee was paid to the people who responded; moreover, the fourteen-page questionnaire required a good deal of time, energy, and commitment to complete.

The information presented in this book is based on 150 responses. Of the respondents, 134, or 89 percent, were women; 16, or 11 percent, were men. Their average age was thirty-seven. In addition, 127, or 85 percent, were white; 20, or 13 percent, were black; and 3, or 2 percent, came from other racial or ethnic groups. A well-educated group of people, 51, or 34 percent, held a graduate degree; 75, or 50 percent, had attended college or completed an undergraduate degree; and only 24, or 16 percent, had a high school education or less. Names, addresses, and telephone numbers were provided by 107 of them, or 71 percent, indicating their willingness to be contacted for a possible follow-up letter or phone call.

While this may seem like a small sample of people, their responses are simply meant to shed light on the taboo of sibling abuse. Their words are unforgettable, and they beg the question of just how much sibling abuse goes on unheeded.

Some people may find the comments of the victims harsh, crude, and even vulgar. They should remember that these are the words of the *victims* of physical, emotional, or sexual abuse. They are telling their stories not to entertain or please anyone, but to describe the pain and the emotional suffering they experienced as children at the hands of their own siblings. Other people may doubt or deny the truth of their statements. Yet there is no logical reason for anyone to go through the trouble of requesting a research questionnaire and then falsify answers to it. To deny the truth of these statements by survivors is to treat sibling abuse the way we have historically treated sexual abuse—by discounting the reality of such abuse and by blaming the child as though he or she wanted the sexual contact in the first place.

Those readers who have children of their own may find this book helpful. The accounts of the survivors—how they were physically, emotionally, or sexually abused by their siblings—may allow parents to recognize the subtle and sometimes not-so-subtle forms of sibling abuse that may exist in their own families. The ways that victims tried to ask for help could be particularly important reading. Becoming sensitive to the various forms of sibling abuse may prompt parents to take action to stop such abuse, or to prevent it from occurring.

All the forms of sibling abuse—physical, emotional, and sexual—are explored in this book. In addition, parental reactions, effects on the victims, and a basic framework for understanding sibling abuse are also examined. Criteria used to distinguish between sibling abuse and sibling rivalry, and strategies for preventing sibling abuse are covered as well. And, lastly, the concluding chapter, "A Final Word," is written, in part, for and to the survivors of sibling abuse. While this book is not expressly directed at them, hopefully it will help them realize that they are not alone, and that the nightmare of their childhood, what happened to them, was not their fault. The comments of the survivors as they speak out may encourage others to seek help if they are still struggling with the long-term effects of sibling abuse.

Sibling abuse may be happening in many American families. Just as education and legislation have successfully dealt with other forms of intra-family violence, similar efforts must now be made to combat sibling abuse. One respondent to the research questionnaire made a plea for this:

> Thanks for being interested in sibling abuse. Those of us who have been victims of this have had to live with it as if we deserved it or it was our fault. My childhood was horrible because of what my brother did to me. I recently met someone whose sister abused her. It was only because I finally sought therapy for my problems that I could talk to her about the abuse both of us received from our siblings. Please get the message out that there is such a thing as sibling abuse.

2

Physical Abuse

Picture this scene: A child is rushed into an emergency room, his face bruised and bleeding. Questioned about the child's injuries, his mother replies that her husband hit the boy. Under law, an attending emergency room staff member must file a report with the local child protective agency. This report triggers an investigation of the father for child abuse, and that, in turn, leads to the prosecution of one or both parents.

Now, suppose the same child is brought to the same emergency room with the same wounds. His mother again is asked about his injuries. She says that the boy's brother smacked him. No report is filed, no investigation takes place, and the case is closed.

Why does this happen? Simply put, it happens because our country's laws do not protect one sibling from another, even when serious abuse occurs. In fact, the law can only protect children from their brothers and sisters if their parents file assault charges against the abusive offspring.

What is meant by "the physical abuse of one sibling by another"? For the purposes of this book, it is defined the following way:

> Physical abuse consists of willful acts resulting in physical injury such as slapping, hitting, biting, kicking, or more violent behavior that may include the use of an instrument, such as a stick, bat, gun, or knife.

The people who completed the research questionnaire that forms the basis for this book used this definition as a guide for their answers. Based on this information, it is clear that the survivors of sibling abuse were victims of a wide range of physically abusive behaviors.

As survivors speak out about physical abuse—even life-threatening forms of abuse—two facts become obvious. First, while society recognizes the physical abuse of children by adults, it closes its eyes to the same abuse when it occurs between children. Second, steps must be taken nationwide to protect children from their siblings, just as they are already protected from their parents.

The Frequency of Physical Abuse

How often does physical abuse by a sibling occur? Based on comments and diaries kept for a week in another study, one researcher found a high level of physical violence between siblings in fifty-seven randomly selected families. Similarly, a survey of 2,143 families showed that sibling violence occurs more frequently than either parent–child or husband–wife violence. In fact, researchers from this last survey estimate that 53 out of 100 children attack a brother or sister every year. Likewise, a study reported by *U. S. News & World Report* found that 138,000 children aged three to seventeen used a weapon on a sibling over a one-year period. If such attacks had occurred outside the family, they would have been considered criminal assaults. Because they took place between brothers and sisters, they were legally ignored.

The Nature of Sibling Physical Abuse

According to responses to the questionnaire, there are roughly three types of sibling physical abuse: (1) hitting, biting, slapping, shoving, and punching; (2) tickling; and (3) life-threatening actions like smothering, choking, and being shot with a BB gun. Often, victims are at the receiving end of more than one of these abuses. And, while "life-threatening" abuse is in a category by itself, the other forms of physical abuse also may have very serious consequences.

The Most Common Forms

The most common forms of physical abuse reported were hitting, slapping, pushing, punching, biting, hair-pulling, scratching, and pinching. Questionnaire respondents had been hit with broom handles, rubber hoses, coat hangers, hairbrushes, belts, and sticks. Some were threatened and stabbed with broken glass, knives, razor blades, and scissors.

The earliest memory of a forty-year-old woman from Kentucky is of being abused by a sibling:

> When I was three or four, my brother pushed me down some stone steps. I had approximately thirty stitches in my knee.

As she grew up, this same woman was often "roughed up" by her two older brothers:

> My brothers typically slugged me in the arm. I was not to cry or everyone went to their rooms. The other favorite activity was to play scissors, paper, and stone. My wrist would be stinging from the hits when I lost. My older brother would usually hit me in the stomach, push me down on the floor, and hold me down while he continued to hit me in the stomach and on the arms.

A New Mexico woman described her older brother's favorite abuse:

> He would engage me in wrestling matches daily, typically punching me in the stomach until I could not breathe, torturing my joints— wrists, knees, and fingers—spitting on me, putting his knees on my arms, and pinning me down and beating on my chest with his knuckles.

A Wisconsin woman, forty-two years old, vividly recalled the treatment she got from two older brothers:

> I remember frequently being curled up in a living room chair with my hands over my face being hit over and over. I usually ended up on the floor and not moving or making noises so they would go away.

Another respondent wrote:

> My sister would hit, kick, or spit on me. Although she was only one year older, she was always much stronger and bigger than me.

A survivor from Maine:

> I can't ever remember not being physically abused by my brother. He beat on me every day. It was just part of existing to me. He would

punch, pinch, and kick me. Sometimes he would pull out my hair. Sometimes he would use weapons or anything else close.

A female survivor from Kansas wrote that her older brother

would start by taking jabs at my face and force me into a corner or until I fell over something and was down. Then he would pound at my shoulders until I cried or pleaded for him to stop, usually telling him I would do his work for him.

Sometimes physical abuse is a learned behavior, passed like a terrible heirloom from parent to child. A Missouri man described being abused by his brother in the same manner practiced by his parents:

Usually the abuse would consist of getting beat up by my brother with his fists or being slapped around with the inside of his hands—a practice he learned from our parents—along with being kicked in the rear.

Often, the abuse got worse in the heat of the moment, as a survivor from Massachusetts revealed:

The abuse consisted usually of my brother punching me in the arms, stomach, back, etc. Usually it started out with a verbal fight, but sometimes he just began punching me if I wouldn't do what he told me to or if he wanted to watch something different on TV. Sometimes things were worse. Once he tried to hit me with an aluminum baseball bat. When I ran away and locked myself in the bathroom, he kicked a hole in the door.

Another respondent:

A minor argument would erupt into violence when I wouldn't do what my brother wanted me to or I wouldn't agree with his opinion. I was shaken, hit, kicked, and slapped. I was never badly hurt, but the level of my brother's rage was such that I was always afraid of it. I knew what was happening was wrong, but I don't think I thought of it as abuse at the time. I've blocked my memories of these events for many years and still don't have all of them back.

One woman wrote that the abuse she suffered from an older brother increased in fury and intensity over the years:

It was mostly my brother, who is five years older than me, that did all the abuse. I would usually be playing by myself somewhere. He would barge in mad or drunk or both, and he'd want me to either get something for him or cook for him. When I would say no, he'd get extremely angry and start hitting me, cursing at me, kicking me, or pushing me around in a total frenzy of violence. It started out by slapping, pushing, cursing. The older we got, the more severe it got. I have suffered from a broken nose and collarbone, and countless bruises and scratches. I still have a BB in my leg where he shot at me. He kicked me with steel-toed boots on my upper arm, and it was red and purple for weeks. I thought he had broken it.

An Unusual Form of Physical Abuse

Tickling is an unusual form of physical abuse engaged in by siblings. Generally not regarded as physical abuse, tickling can, in fact, become abusive under certain conditions.

Tickling involves two people—one who does the tickling, and one who is being tickled. Tickling can be enjoyable when it occurs in a context of trust and mutual respect. In such cases, the person being tickled knows it will stop on request. However, while it can be pleasant—even erotic—it also can be painful. The nerve fibers that respond to tickling are the same ones that respond to pain.

Tickling becomes painful and abusive if the person being tickled has no control over the situation. When tickling continues despite pleas for it to stop, it is abusive. Some people, siblings in this case, pin their victims to the floor in order to tickle them. As the victims are usually smaller than their more aggressive siblings, they are often helpless and cannot fight back. This is true of most sibling physical abuse.

Several people had serious reactions to being tickled. An Ohio woman, forty-eight, reported that her older sister would punch and slap her, and then pin her down on the floor before tickling her until she vomited.

Another woman was repeatedly tickled by her older brother. Her brother, who was very strong, would kneel on her arms as he slapped and tickled her. She was powerless to resist. Later, her feelings of lying submissive and helpless on the floor became symbolic of her adult interactions:

I became a doormat in my other relationships with men. It made me very timid and shy and left me with no self-esteem.

Another woman wrote that she had recently attended a seminar where tickling was mentioned as a form of physical abuse. She already knew that she had been a victim of her siblings, through this and other behaviors, but felt that her parents and society in general expected her to accept this as typical child's play. She remembered:

> I was unmercifully tickled by my brother, who held down every limb and body part that wiggled and covered my mouth when I cried and yelled for help. He pulled my hair after I pulled his, thinking that would hurt him and he would stop.

This survivor's mother ignored her son's behavior by saying he was being playful, despite her daughter's tears and protestations. This abuse continues to affect her in her adult years. She does not like to be touched by other people, especially when they put their hands around her waist, or hold her in any way that reminds her of being restrained.

A Missouri woman, who was abusively tickled by an older brother and sister, reacted in a similar way:

> My brother and sister would hold me down and tickle me until I cried. They considered this play and would usually do it when my parents were gone. They would finally let me go and then laugh because I was a "crybaby." On one occasion I told my mother what they did, and she scolded them but told me they were just playing.

Life-Threatening Abuse

What begins as normal play among siblings can escalate into aggression, and can result in injury. At one time or another most children have been injured—often accidentally—by a sibling while playing. However, these are rare or isolated incidents. Several points are helpful in separating such common childhood events from those described later on.

First of all, abusive incidents are commonplace or repeated. In abusive situations, a particular behavior or event may have happened only once, but it was *typical* of how a sibling treated his or her victim.

Second, how siblings react to causing injuries also must be considered. In most abusive instances, siblings laughed at their victims. This response further "injured" victims because it made them believe their siblings *wanted* to hurt them. Behavior that accidentally leads to harm is usually followed by an immediate apology— not one demanded by parents or baby-sitters.

Finally, how parents react to abuse between their children should be examined. When children are hurt by siblings while playing, parents generally comfort and take care of them. Parents also might discipline siblings who caused the problem, or discuss it with them. At the very least, parents may make an attempt to find out what happened. But when parents shrug their shoulders, deny that victims are in pain, or blame the victims for what happened, the event has become doubly abusive.

One woman described an episode that happened when she was six or seven years old that was typical of the behavior of her siblings. It was the earliest in a long series of abusive events, but it remains vivid in her memory: her two brothers grabbed her by her legs and arms, swung her around three times, then let her fly off into a hedge of thornbushes.

Two other incidents were recalled by a woman fifty-five years old. They left physical scars that remain to this day.

> I climbed on the chicken coop and a nail penetrated my foot. It went all the way through my foot. I was literally nailed to the coop. My older sister saw me and laughed and told me that's what I deserved. She left and wouldn't help me down. After a long time my older brother came by, helped me get down, and took me to the hospital for help and a tetanus shot. I was so afraid I would get lockjaw. I still have the scar on my foot. Once my sister was ironing. She was a teenager; I was between four and five. I was curious as to what she was doing. I put my hands flat up on the ironing board, and she immediately put the hot iron down on my hand. She laughed and told me to get lost. I still have the burn scar on my left hand.

BB guns were another life-threatening form of abuse reported in the questionnaires:

> My younger brother was playing April Fools' jokes, so one of my older brothers aimed a BB gun at him and shot him. He said "April Fools"

and started laughing. My younger brother was lying on the ground in a lot of pain.

One survivor commented:

My brothers would chase me into an open field and shoot BBs from a gun at me. I was hit in the ankle.

A Nevada respondent, often abused by her brother, lost an eye after he aimed and shot her in the face with a BB gun.

Another woman in her late forties described her older brother's abuse, and her parents' response to it:

When I was two or three, my mother went to visit my father, who was in the Army, and my brother and I were left in the care of my grandparents. My brother was helping my grandfather paint a fence and painted me from head to toe with dark brown paint. The paint was in my hair, face, clothing, etc., and I had to be scrubbed down with turpentine and repeated baths. Some of my hair had to be cut to get the paint out. My brother laughed and teased me about all this. Later, during another incident, my brother wrote his name on my bare back with his wood-burning kit. He seemed to treat me as an object rather than as a person with any feelings. My abuse continued through high school. My brother would twist my arms, or pin me down, and bend my arms or legs to get me to do things he wanted me to do, such as his chores or to cover for him by lying to my parents. These incidents usually happened when my parents weren't home. When I reported them to my parents, he would say I was making it up to get him in trouble. Then we would both be punished. I knew my parents didn't know how to handle the problem, so I quit reporting to them. I would just arrange to go to a friend's house or have a friend over when my parents were going to be out.

A respondent from California wrote:

My brother discovered that hitting in the solar plexus caused one to black out. So he would hit me and watch me pass out.

Even when incidents don't result in injuries, they may still be—or feel—abusive and life-threatening. Many people reported having been "jokingly" strangled by an older sibling. While it may have been in fun, the victims still went through the terror, fright, and anxiety of having their air cut off—even if it was momentary. A forty-year-old Texas woman noted:

I have photographs of my brother pushing me down and trying to "playfully" strangle me when I was an infant.

When she was four to six years old, the woman's brother often pretended he was going to choke her to death. The effects of this abuse have lingered, leaving her very frightened of men and terrified of anyone touching her neck. Because of her past, she is unwilling to have more than one child.

Another Texan who described herself as extremely afraid of people—particularly men—endured a similar, and calculated kind of abuse from her older brother:

My oldest brother would put his arms around my chest tight and not let me inhale any air while I had to watch in the mirror as he laughed and explained how I was going to die.

Likewise, another survivor:

Under the guise of "play-fighting," my older brother would choke me until I was gagging. As he got older and stronger, this got more vicious. He also brutalized other kids smaller than he was.

Smothering seems to be another popular, and life-threatening form of sibling abuse. One survivor wrote:

I remember my brother putting a pillow over my head. He would hold it and laugh while I struggled to get out from under him and the pillow. I remember being terrified. I honestly thought he would smother me to death. This occurred frequently. Once, all three of my brothers put a pillow over my face, and I couldn't breathe. I struggled as much as I could to get away. What stopped them was, my mom was coming up the driveway.

One woman wrote that her brother, who was four years older than she was,

put a pillow over my face and smothered me until I almost died. He was twice my size and very big. One time I did pass out, and I came to when he gave me mouth-to-mouth resuscitation.

A male respondent from Oregon described the abuse he received from an older brother:

Sometimes he would choke me with his hands or pin me down with a pillow over my face. The first time he did this was when I was four years old.

A survivor from Washington explained:

My brother forced me to the bottom of my sleeping bag and held the top closed so I couldn't get out or breathe. When I realized I couldn't get out, I became panic-stricken and thought I was going to die. Even as I write this, I am taken back to that moment and feel just the way I felt then. As an adult, I'm claustrophobic and can't have my face covered without panic setting in.

A Louisiana respondent was particularly vulnerable to a potentially deadly form of abuse devised by his four older siblings:

I don't remember when it started, but my brothers and sisters used to hit me in the stomach to knock the breath out of me because I had asthma and they thought it was funny to see me wheeze. I was around four or five years of age. Also, my sisters and brothers would hit me in the nose to make me sneeze and count the number of times I would sneeze. Whoever made me sneeze most was the winner. Once I sneezed seventeen times. On another occasion I bled from my nose all over a new chair my parents had bought after my brother hit me in the nose.

Drowning is another form of abuse that can be fatal. It was suffered by a New Yorker with one sibling—a brother who was three years older:

My brother made several serious attempts to drown me in local pools and later laughed about it. These attempts continued until I was strong enough to get away and could swim.

An Iowa woman, who described numerous vicious attacks by her older siblings, reported her earliest memory of physical abuse:

I was three or four years old. My family went camping often. We were out at a little lake. I was walking with my two brothers. We walked out on a dock to see the ducks closer, and my brothers pushed me in the water. I couldn't swim! They just stood on the dock and laughed at me. I was gasping for air. I thought I was going to die! Then the next thing I remember is someone pulling me out. It was a farmer driving by on his tractor. He took us all back to camp, and he told my parents he had pulled me out. I told my parents that my brothers had pushed me, and they said I fell in.

Whether or not injury results, the effects of physical abuse can be long lasting. Chapter 7 discusses this aspect of all forms of sibling abuse.

The Power Motif

Why would brothers and sisters—or anyone at all—do such things to one another? Although chapter 6 more closely examines this question, one constant element in these events deserves to be identified immediately. It is common to child abuse, spouse abuse, sibling abuse, and, arguably, numerous other crimes committed by strangers instead of family members. It is power. Abuse is the awful fast-track to achieving power and control, and it lies at the heart of not only physical abuse but also emotional and sexual abuse. An Illinois woman recognized this theme in her brother's abusive actions:

> He would punch me with his closed fists in the arms or back. Usually this occurred around issues of him dominating me. He would resort to physical abuse to dominate me.

Perpetrators, or abusers, feel the need to dominate, or have power and control. They may try to take charge because they feel powerless—or less worthy than their victims—for a variety of reasons. For example, abusers may think that their victims get more parental attention, receive better grades in school, have more friends, or are more attractive. From that insecure perspective, they may use force as a way to bolster or increase their low self-esteem.

Physical force was used by one older sister to gain control of this female survivor from Indiana:

> My sister would be instantly angry over seemingly little incidents. If her assault of words didn't bring about what she thought was a submissive response, she became violent with her hands and fists. She would slap my face, arms, and shoulders.

Most of the abusive events detailed in this book were performed by males. In fact, 134, or 89 percent, of the 150 respondents were female, and in the majority of cases they were abused by a brother or brothers. There are two perhaps equally valid theories to support these statistics showing the female-as-victim. One is that fewer males responded to the research because—bowing to traditional male upbringing, or socialization—men find it harder to admit they are out of control, or are victims of someone more powerful than themselves. Male survivors may also have more difficulty seeking counseling, which makes it less likely that they would respond to the ad for the questionnaire. If so, then male survivors share some traits with male abusers, who seem to believe maleness, or masculinity, equals control and power. In short, the same upbringing that left some boys silent survivors, made their brothers become abusers.

Power appears to be a male-oriented issue in today's society. Many men still mistakenly believe that they must be in control. Feeling powerless creates problems for some of them. They think they are *expected* to be powerful, and they seek to satisfy that idea. They try to get that sense of power by putting females—in this case their sibling sisters—in physically powerless situations. Power-seeking is the framework for males becoming perpetrators and their sisters victims. The sense of power and control that they get from being abusive makes them want to repeat the experience. It meets a need for the male who feels weak, but, unfortunately, it is a need that can never be completely fulfilled. Boys also gain power and control over their sisters through emotional and sexual abuse, issues that will be explored later in this book.

Still another possibility, also related to socialization, is that older sisters are more likely to be expected to take care of younger siblings. They are expected to nurture and protect their little brothers or sisters. Older brothers, on the other hand, may not receive that same kind of message from their parents, or society in general.

How Victims Respond

How do victims respond to being physically abused? Typically, they protect themselves, cry and scream, run away, become abusive themselves, or tell their parents.

Protecting Themselves

Most often, children respond to physical abuse by protecting themselves. A young woman from New York described how she tried to shield herself from a sister who was a year older:

> My sister would beat me up, and I would sit on my bed with my knees up guarding myself until she stopped.

Screaming and Crying

Another natural reaction to physical abuse is to cry for help. Sadly, this response often provokes even more furious physical attacks.

The following incident may spur similar memories in many readers. An older brother is beating a younger sibling. When the child cries or screams for help, the beating intensifies. The older boy warns, "Take it like you should!" or "If you cry, I'll give you more!" Unfortunately, both children may have learned this unfair response from their parents. Most people have either witnessed or experienced a parent spanking a child and yelling, "If you don't stop crying, I'll really give you something to cry about!"

The activity between parent and child, and between siblings, is identical. The victim's natural response is to cry or call for help, but that may result in more abuse or more punishment. The victim is in a catch-22 situation.

One survivor described this dilemma:

My brother was very violent—quick to anger, quick to strike out. He would slap, hit, kick, or trip me. If I reacted negatively, he would become more violent and use his size and strength to hurt me—that is, punch me in the face or shove me.

A Tennessee respondent wrote:

My brother would begin by hitting, biting, or placing a pillow over my face. He would demand that I say uncle or beg him to stop. When I did so, he only hurt me more. If I didn't do what he said, he'd hurt me more. I was in a no-win situation. I felt helpless because I was helpless.

An Indiana woman attempted to escape from her brother, which only resulted in more violence.

When I tried to run away, he would chase me until he could grab my hair and pull me to a stop.

Fleeing the Abuser

Finding themselves in powerless, vulnerable positions, many victims responded in the only way they could: they physically separated themselves from their abusers and hid to avoid further harassment.

Victims locked themselves in their bedrooms if they were lucky enough to have their own rooms; or spent as much time as possible away from home, with friends.

One woman protected herself from her brother this way:

> I became a very withdrawn child. I would retreat to my room and read. If my brother was involved in a game, I wouldn't play. If he was in a particular room, I would go to a different one.

Another woman, who, along with her younger siblings, was tormented by an older sister while growing up, discovered a unique way to put an end to the abuse.

> She would yell and scream and chase us around. She would swing her arms at us and hit any part of us she could. I'd curl up in a ball and cover my head in my arms when she caught me. Often I was lucky enough to run away from her and hide. One day I was playing in the basement with a small snake when she came after me. She saw the snake and ran away in fear. After that I really liked snakes and tried to have one with me as often as I could for protection against her rage.

A woman of forty-four was a frequent victim of her older brother's physical abuse. She coped by trying to keep out of his way.

> I would try to stay away from him, but if he caught me, I wouldn't say or do anything. I was afraid he would just get angrier if I made a fuss. I tried telling my parents, but they always believed my brother. I didn't tell them anymore.

Another woman, thirty-four, experienced daily doses of abuse from her only brother. She handled it this way:

> My brother would hit me, bite me, wrestle me, etc., anytime my parents were out of sight. The times that were most frightening for me were after school—the period between when we arrived home from school and when my parents came home from work—about two to three hours. I would run to my room and lock the door, or go to a friend's house so he wouldn't terrorize me.

A survivor of physical abuse levied by an older sister reported:

> I didn't dare cry because no one believed me anyway. Most of the time, I just got away from her and hid.

A Montana woman who was physically abused by her brother reported that he always played games in which she was his victim. One game he favored, which readers may remember from their childhoods, was "Flinch." Her brother, who was seven years older than she was, would pretend to slap her face. If she blinked, he would hit her on the arm. If she didn't flinch the first time, he would keep trying until she did, and then would hit her twice because he claimed he got bonus points. He also invented the game "Tickle Torture," in which he would tickle her until she wet her pants or couldn't breathe. Still another variation was called "Crab People," in which he would pinch her, leaving bruises on her body. The victim recognized how helpless she was, and dealt with her abuse in the best way she knew.

> My brother was so much bigger; it was impossible to retaliate. He would hurt me, and it would make me angry. I tried to hurt back, but it was useless. I was too small. My hits were nothing, and he was likely to try something else. It was better to hide.

In general, victims of sibling abuse live in constant fear of further battering. Attempts to scream or cry out for help are often either futile or seen as invitations for more abuse. Hiding is the only way some victims find to cope with the problem. As children, life involves—and self-protection depends on—sensing the mood of an abusive sibling. A woman from Maine, thirty-nine years old, was the victim of an older brother's physical abuse:

> I learned to sense his bad moods and dreaded being left alone with him at any time, as he seemed always to find some reason to hurt me.

When the Abused Become Abusers

Sadly, some victims of sibling physical abuse responded by heaping the same sort of abuse on younger, even weaker siblings. Using their abusers' behavior as a model, these victims learned to become perpetrators, taking out their frustrations on those unable to fight back. Anna Freud, in her well-known book *The Ego and the Mechanisms of Defense,* calls this response a "psychological defense" and labels it an "identification with the aggressor." A continuing, dominolike pattern is created, and unless parents intervene, abuse of weaker siblings by stronger ones may become commonplace. A young woman described the process in this way:

> The worst fights started around the time I was in third grade. I got a lot of abuse from my older brother. Then I would turn around and abuse my sister. I would get her twice as hard as what I received. As we got older it got worse. I would have knives pulled on me. Then I would turn around and pull a gun on one of the others. I would take my anger out on my sister or younger brother. I became very violent, especially toward my sister.

Telling Their Parents

Many victims do tell their parents they are being abused by a sibling, but this response doesn't always help matters. In fact, the abusers often use the crime of "telling" as an excuse to punish their victims even more. Parents often blame victims for the physical abuse they report. "You must have done something to deserve it," parents might say. Such remarks not only don't protect victims, they discourage victims from telling their parents about any other abuses. Another common response is for parents to become very angry and physically discipline both abusers and victims. This reaction has the same effect of discouraging victims from reporting physical abuse.

Certainly, many children who are physically abused by a sibling do tell their parents, and their parents do intervene appropriately. The intervention may involve discussing the event with the siblings, determining what provoked the abuse, perhaps identifying how each sibling contributed to the incident, and helping them consider other, nonviolent ways the issue could have been handled. This problem-solving approach is an effective way for parents to intervene in sibling abuse situations. Discussed more fully in chapter 5, this approach teaches siblings to effectively handle interpersonal problems without resorting to abuse or violence, and allows the parents to give a clear message that abusive behavior will not be tolerated. Obviously, many parents try to use this or other, similar methods to deal with problems between their children. However, the respondents to the questionnaire often found that their parents reacted in ways that were ineffective, leaving them open to more abuse. Even as adults, years after the abuses occurred, many continue to feel like victims.

Physical Abuse Is Not Alone

Most of the time physical abuse by a sibling does not occur in a vacuum; it is accompanied by emotional and sexual abuse. In fact, a combination of physical, emotional, and sexual abuse was reported by 107, or 71 percent, of the 150 people answering the questionnaire. This is discussed more fully at the end of the next chapter. However, the following brief comments illustrate the problem.

Along with the name-calling, there were the beatings I got from my brother.

My brother would try to get me to do things to him sexually, and when I refused, he beat me till I did.

I remember the physical abuse—hitting, choking, rough force, hitting my head against things and tearing at my clothes—which he used to force me to engage in sexual activities.

Physical abuse between siblings can have terrible long-term effects on its victims. Emotional abuse, the subject of the following chapter, is harder to detect both when it is occurring and later but has equally devastating results.

3

Emotional Abuse

"Sticks and stones may break my bones, but words will never hurt me." It's a common refrain among children. No one knows who invented the jingle, but it's been passed down from generation to generation like some valuable piece of truth. But is it true?

The survivors of emotional abuse are best equipped to answer that question, and they do so in the pages that follow. They tell of names they were called, and of the ridicule and verbal degradation they received. They relate how their personal possessions were destroyed, and how their pets were tortured or killed. The emotional abuse they suffered as children still affects most of them as adults. Their experiences are proof that the old jingle not only is untrue but also promotes the false idea that emotional abuse should not hurt.

What Is Emotional Abuse?

Emotional abuse is often thrown in under the vast, and false, cloak of teasing. In fact, many victims of emotional abuse frequently note that they were "teased" by a sibling. While teasing can suggest a little gentle kidding or playful banter, it also has become a catch-all word meaning to belittle, ridicule, intimidate, annoy, scorn, provoke, and harass.

Teasing should be distinguished from joking. For the purposes of this book, teasing involves a perpetrator and a victim, and it occurs at the victim's expense; joking involves a more equal relationship between two people. It can revolve around people and topics other than the victim. Laughter, rather than emotional pain, is usually the result of joking.

Researchers believe that emotional abuse, or psychological maltreatment, is both more common and perhaps more destructive than other forms of child abuse and neglect. In fact, the federal Child Abuse Prevention and Treatment Act of 1974 labels emotional abuse as a "mental injury."

Identifying Emotional Abuse

Emotional abuse is difficult to identify. There are no laws to help prove that it existed in one case or another, and no standards to help determine how serious it may have been. Further, unlike physical and sexual abuse, emotional abuse doesn't leave any real evidence behind—no visible scrapes, cuts, bruises, or stained and torn clothing. That same hidden quality of emotional abuse may also make it harder for family, friends, teachers, mental health professionals, and even parents to recognize it in children.

One reason emotional abuse is so hard to detect is that professionals and parents often confuse it with normal behavior among children. Teasing and verbal "put-downs" are common weapons among children, and thus may be excused by parents as sibling rivalry.

Unfortunately, when parents excuse or overlook emotional abuse between their children, victims often believe that their treatment is not really abusive. After all, if the behavior was abusive, then Mom or Dad would do something about it, wouldn't they? As a result, survivors often deny that what happened was abusive. As a woman from Kentucky put it:

> When asked if I was emotionally abused by a sibling, my inclination is to say no, that it was not significant. However, I used to say the same thing about sexual abuse.

Incidence of Emotional Abuse

The questionnaire asked people to identify how often they were emotionally abused while growing up. Their responses indicate that such treatment was routine in their relationships with their siblings and, in some cases, with their parents. One survivor commented that she was aware that all siblings make snide remarks to one another, but that "the frequency and intensity of these" made for an abnormal relationship with her older brother. Many respondents described a constant flow of emotional abuse. For these people, their childhoods were filled with name-calling, ridicule, and mockery.

A woman from Illinois responded:

I was constantly being told I was no good, a pig, whore, slut, all sexually oriented negatives. I was constantly being degraded emotionally.

A survivor from Maine:

I can't remember a time when I was growing up when my brother didn't taunt me.

A respondent from Virginia:

He constantly teased me about my appearance—every aspect of it— and everything I did.

A woman in her late thirties:

I don't ever remember not being teased or made to cry. I was always called names.

An Ohio resident:

From my earliest memories, age five or so, my siblings called me names and said degrading things to me.

A mother of several children recalled her relationship with her older brother:

He constantly berated me verbally, calling me names like "worthless," "slut," "pig."

Many people's earliest memories of emotional abuse dated from age four or five. The abuse may have started earlier than that, but that is as far back as they can remember. For these people, emotional abuse by a sibling was a way of life. One woman's description of her relationship with her older brother shows how this works:

Let me put it this way; in my baby book, my mother wrote, "Mary's first words were—Sam, don't."

She said that her brother hated her from the day she was born and behaved accordingly.

Types of Emotional Abuse

Emotional abuse can take on many different forms. In this book, emotional abuse has been broken down into the following categories: name-calling, ridicule, degradation, promoting a fear, destroying personal possessions, and torture or destruction of a pet. This list is not complete—nor does its suggest that one type of abuse is worse than another—it simply identifies the most common types of emotional abuse.

The first three—name-calling, ridicule, and degradation—are usually referred to as teasing. They have been given more accurate, and less kind, names here so that parents and professionals can better recognize them as abusive.

Name-Calling

Name-calling is the most common form of emotional abuse. Nearly every person who reported being emotionally abused made some comment about being called names. Such names are usually belittling or degrading, and often focus on things like victims' height, weight, hair, face, intelligence, whether or not they were athletic or could perform certain skills, and so on. For example, an Arkansas woman's brothers called her "fatso" and "roly-poly." Another victim's dry skin prompted her siblings to call her "snake" and "crocodile."

One survivor wrote:

When I was six, my mother realized I needed glasses. For the next several years my brothers told me I was ugly and taunted me with a lot of names referring to being unattractive.

Another stated:

I was told that I was stupid and ugly and usually called "ugly" as a name.

A woman in Montana also grew up being called names by her siblings:

I was heavy as a young child, about seven or eight years old. My brother called me "cow." He was asked to mark all the children's socks with our names, so for mine he drew the face of a cow. He would take a mistake I made and turn it into a nasty word game that he would call at me for years. I once put on a halter top and due to the design, I put it on sideways. Then he called me "the sideways girl." He called me a Spanish word which I understood meant "whore." A mistake was for a lifetime.

Someone else wrote:

My brother, four years older than me, would tease, taunt, and call me names. He often did this in front of me or his friends, the latter of whom were encouraged to join in.

Sadly, many survivors feel less confident and worthwhile as people because of this abuse. "Stupid," "dumb," and "ugly" were favorite names used to describe them. One victim of two older sisters wrote:

I would be told by one or both of my sisters I was dumb and ugly and that's why I didn't have many friends to play with like they did.

A Washington respondent noted:

My sister would verbally harass me—you're ugly, stupid, fat, and so on. If I did accomplish something, she would turn things around and prove that I had failed or been a fool.

A male survivor from Ohio:

I was left-handed and could not throw a ball very well. When we played softball in our neighborhood, my older brothers never wanted me to play on their teams. I was called names because of this. When they chose sides, they would never want me. Many times I would be left out of the game and would go home because they didn't want me. Of course, neither my brothers nor anyone else would help me learn to properly throw a ball. The same was true for coaches who taught gym classes. Their only concern was to win, win, win! To this day I hate sports! I thought a coach's job was to help you learn sports. When I hear the word *sports* or *coach* today, I want to puke.

Ridicule

Ridicule is a way to express contempt. When combined with an abuser's laughter, it can be particularly painful to hear. A young woman wrote:

My sister would get her friends to sing songs about how ugly I was.

Another survivor wrote that her older sister composed a song about her and the fact that she was overweight. Her sister sang the song, which rhymed, whenever she was near her. The target of all this "wit" was further humiliated when her sister sang the song in front of friends at school who joined in the fun and laughter.

One survivor of emotional abuse in her early thirties was laughed at so often as a child that she still does not speak up for herself.

My brother would tease me about not saying certain words correctly. Some words I could not pronounce correctly, so he would get me to say them and then would laugh at me. [Now] I feel like people will laugh at what I have to say or they will think it's dumb.

Another survivor was abused by an older brother in this way:

It consisted mostly of mindless ridicule—"You're ugly"; "Your hair is frizzy"; "You're going to school looking like that?" The abuse usually occurred when we were alone or in front of the family.

A woman from Indiana suffered ridicule from a sister who was two years older. High school provided the backdrop for her worst years of abuse:

If we were riding around town and a boy or boys would wave, I'd wave back, and she would begin a battery of insults. "Why did you wave? Never wave at anybody when I'm in the car. They wouldn't wave at you anyway. You are scar face, crooked tooth, dumpy, and ugly. No one wants to wave at you," and on and on she would go. She would criticize me in front of her friends—not simply verbal attempts but a battery of verbal assaults, as if my living on earth were enough to make me deserve it. Her friends laughed, which brought on more despair for me. I internalized this incessant criticism as something for which I was responsible.

Often, a sibling's name is used as a tool of ridicule. One woman wrote that she was called "sewer" because her first name was Sue and her last name began with a W. The name she had been given by her parents—a name over which she had no control—was repeatedly used against her by her siblings.

Ridicule often has sexual overtones. A Kentucky woman, emotionally abused by her brothers, explained:

> There was much teasing of a sexual nature from my brothers as I was going through puberty. Great fun was made of my wearing a bra and putting cotton in it. When I started menses, I would hide used Kotex in my radio so they would not tease me.

A woman from Idaho, forty-eight years old, still vividly remembers the emotional abuse she received in her family of thirteen children. She was repeatedly ridiculed about her appearance. When she was eight years old, she lost a front tooth, and the new tooth came in crooked and diseased. When she was twelve, she gained weight.

> Between the two, I was under fire constantly—ugly, fat, rotten tooth, etc., and the freckles didn't help!

Another person wrote:

> Life as a child consisted of constant taunts and ridicule on issues such as things I said, clothes I wore, my friends, etc.

Summarizing her abuse, a Washington woman noted:

> I was ridiculed by my older brothers and sisters for just being. Ridicule and put-downs were "normal" for our family.

Degradation

Degradation is another type of emotional abuse aimed at depriving individuals of their sense of dignity and value. Victims are often told they are "worthless" and "no good." These messages are devastating to the victims at the time, and may continue to haunt them as adults, according to the people who responded to the questionnaire. This seems particularly true for people whose parents ignored or accepted the abuse or, worse still, joined in on it.

Children who degrade their siblings or peers probably don't realize how terribly it can affect someone. Abusers may take the old "sticks and stones" jingle as proof that their words missed the target. Or maybe they just don't care.

Imagine the small child whose entire world and sense of security is based on family and peer relationships. He is aware of what others think of him. He wants to be liked, to be valued by his brother and his friends. But his brother keeps telling him he doesn't belong in the family, and that no one really likes him—not his friends or anyone else who knows him.

Children are especially vulnerable to degrading remarks because they have not yet developed a strong, positive sense of self. Abusive siblings tell them they are ugly, or worthless, or dumb. When their parents don't intervene, the victim accepts the message as truth. The victim silently agrees and accepts the abuser's remarks.

A survivor from Washington repeatedly received such a message from an older sister when she was growing up:

> I was being constantly told how ugly, dumb, unwanted I was. Already about two years of age I was told, "No one wants you around. I [my sister] wish you were dead. You aren't my real sister, your parents didn't want you, either, so they dumped you with us." I grew up feeling, if my own family doesn't like me, who will? I believed everything my sister ever told me—that I was ugly, dumb, homely, stupid, fat—even though I always was average in weight. I felt no one would ever love me. When you're little, you believe everything you're told—it can last a lifetime.

A man in his mid-forties is in therapy for the emotional abuse he got from his two older brothers.

> I was told that I was no good, that no one loved me, that I was adopted (which was not true), that my parents did not really want me. My parents were always gone and emotionally unavailable, partially due to alcohol abuse, so that I was often left in the care of my two older brothers.

A California respondent:

> When we were kids, my brother would tell all his friends how ugly I was. He belittled me as long as I can remember.

A young man who identified himself as gay was also degraded by a brother while growing up.

> My brother would tell me what a sissy or faggot I was; that I wasn't a man, and then he would laugh. He would tell others to taunt me, to bait me. He would bring me to tears.

One woman was abused throughout her childhood. Her earliest memory:

> I was about five, and my father was fussing at me about not knowing how to tie my shoes. But no one ever taught me. My brother started laughing at me, telling me I was stupid and dumb and I was not his sister. He said my mother and father found me in a trash can and felt sorry for me and took me to their house. He wished I would go back to the trash can.

When children look different from their siblings, being told they are adopted can take on the scary ring of truth. A Louisiana respondent remembers:

> My brothers and sisters . . . would tell me I was adopted because I had blond hair and fair skin and they were dark skinned and dark haired. They would tell me Mom and Dad wouldn't love me if I told on them.

A respondent from Kansas wrote about the effects of having an emotionally abusive older brother:

> I would cry and feel deeply wounded (after he emotionally abused me by calling me names). I felt for many years that I was adopted because he looked so different, and he was treated so very different than me. I soon adapted my life to do and be the exact opposite of him. He made A's—I got by on C's.

A few short sentences took a devastating toll on a woman whose mother was mentally ill. Her brothers told her:

> "She went crazy after she had you. If it weren't for you, she'd be all right."

Two older brothers inflicted constant emotional abuse on a Kentucky resident, who noted:

My brothers loved to tease me to tears. They were ruthless in their teasing and did not let up. They teased me for being ugly. They teased me for being sloppy. They teased me for just being. This was the worst.

One woman was told in any number of ways that she shouldn't exist—a message that was also acted out by her siblings.

My brothers and cousin tied me to a stake and were preparing the ground around me to set it on fire. They were stopped and built a dummy of me instead and burnt that.

Many people said that their emotional abuse followed them into adulthood. The patterns of abuse that were started in childhood continued even though they were no longer children. Research shows that, sometimes, one child in a family becomes a scapegoat, or is treated as an outsider, and continues to play that role as an adult as well. Things like nicknames can last a lifetime, haunting grown-ups who were abused as children.

A woman in South Carolina, who has formed a support group for adults abused as children, was—and still is—abused by an older brother and sister:

They would tell me things like I was stupid and call me other names, make fun of me, make me do things I did not want to do, beat me up when I didn't do what they wanted. They made me feel I was not part of their family. They showed they loved each other but not me. And they still do this to me the same way, even at thirty-five years old.

A female physician in her forties wrote that the abuse she received from her older brother persists to this day:

I can't recall a specific instance of emotional abuse. It was more of an attitude that still continues today. There is no sensitivity or openness from my brother. As a child I always felt I had to be "nice" and agree, or I would be yelled at or not accepted. As a child he wouldn't think of me as a person. Even now, there is no acknowledgment of me as an adult. But now I pity him more than anything because I see through his macho front and see a very insecure, immature, selfish, weak man who is threatened by my success and assertiveness. He still has a superior attitude. I do see him. Our interactions are not meaningful or support-ive—more formal or "proper." But he still calls me names if he doesn't get his way.

A Massachusetts woman wrote:

My relationship with my brothers and sisters is still somewhat strained. I am out of place with them. Their humor is sarcastic. They make insulting, negative remarks.

Although some survivors heard the same nasty comments over and over, children can be just as devastated by a single vicious remark, made only once. For these people, a particularly awful statement may feel like a physical wound; and while a wound may heal, the pain of an emotionally abusive incident can linger a life-time.

Another way abusers may degrade their siblings is by "using" them. Often happening along male–female lines, brothers lord it over their sisters. For instance, an older brother insists his younger sister complete his household chores. Failure to do so may mean getting beaten up.

Children used in this way said they felt they existed only to do things for an older sibling, as if they were servants. A respondent who was raised on a farm in North Dakota in a very religious family of eight children had to wait on her older brothers in the house, even if she had worked all day in the fields. Her parents told her to obey her older brothers in their absence, leaving her with the feeling that, "It was as if my brothers could do no wrong." The older boys took advantage of her, not only by demanding she do tasks for them, but by tricking her out of her allowance and, eventually, by sexually abusing her.

An Iowa woman was similarly degraded by an older brother:

He'd come home drunk and wake me up in the middle of the night and make me cook for him. I was his personal slave. He'd have a party and make a hell of a mess. I'd have to clean it up.

Again, the theme of male domination runs rampant through the descriptions of all types of abuse—physical, emotional, and sexual. A New Mexico woman, for example, got a lot of attention from her older brother, but it was accompanied by a hefty dose of emotional abuse. The abuse focused on her gender:

He would tease me for being a weak girl. He would taunt me about being sissy. He would delight in teasing me, make me laugh sometimes, and then discard me. It was confusing because I liked the special attention, but it hurt so much.

This woman reported that her abused childhood severely impacted her adult relationships:

I felt guilty bonding with other males and wasn't sure I could trust them. I felt crippling shame. I drank and acted out.

Being ignored is another way children are degraded by their siblings. A West Coast woman felt she was treated that way by her older and younger brothers because she was a girl. The message she received was that she was supposed to take care of them, but not to play or have fun with them. Her brothers tried to force her to stay at home and serve them, and, she noted,

They totally ignored me. They did not want me along or around for anything, ever. They would not talk to me or play with me.

Another respondent, this time from Maine, also was ignored by a sibling:

The worst kind of emotional abuse I experienced was if I walked into a room, my brother would pretend he was throwing up at the sight of me. As I got older, he most often would pretend I wasn't there and would speak as if I didn't exist, even in front of my father and my mother.

When children are given the feeling that they shouldn't exist, they are pawns in what some psychologists call the "Don't Be" game. They are given subtle and not-so-subtle messages that life would be much better if they weren't around—that their parents would have fewer financial woes, or that there would be less tension in the house. Unfortunately, this "game" is extremely destructive. Children don't ask to be born, and they are not responsible for their existence. Realistically, what can they do to fulfill the wish that they didn't exist? Although this game is usually played by parents, it can be equally damaging when acted out by children. Worse still, parents may not stop the abuse when they hear it. One survivor reported that her older and younger brothers told her they wished she didn't exist, and treated her that way. She said her parents just never thought about it or thought that it was harmful. They denied the evidence of my unhappiness and depression.

A Texan's sibling played "Don't Be" with her:

> I was two or three years old, and my parents and my brothers had gone somewhere. I had fallen asleep in the back window of the car. I woke up and was alone in the car. It was raining. I was scared to get out, so I just sat and waited. My oldest brother came out of the house and ran to the car. When he opened the door, he laughed at me because he knew I was scared. He told me my parents hated me and that they had left me there hoping someone would come and kill me. He said he hoped he would get to kill me. Then he told me over and over how he would do it.

Promoting a Fear

Some people who responded to the questionnaire described another form of emotional abuse. Their siblings would take advantage of one of the victim's fears—such as a fear of being lost, a fear of the dark, or a fear of strangers—and increase it. Fear became the tool with which siblings could control their victims and get their own way. Abusive siblings may have learned this manipulative behavior from their parents.

One female victim had an intense fear of a parakeet that the family kept as a pet.

> When we were in elementary school, my sisters would get the parakeet out of the cage and bring it near me. They would put it on my head so it would scratch me.

She panicked when the bird came near her and took to hiding until her siblings grew bored with terrorizing her.

Another respondent wrote that her older brothers would terrify her by taking her to the woods near their home and leaving her to find her own way home.

Fears of being eaten by wild animals and monsters were also played upon by older brothers and sisters. One woman remembers that when she was in first grade, her oldest brother threatened to tie her to a tree and let the wolves eat her. He also warned her repeatedly that he was going to lock her out of the house so that the "bogeyman" would kill her.

A Virginia woman, now in her forties, got similar treatment from her siblings:

> They would take my sister and me out into the field to pick berries. When we would hear dogs barking, they would tell us they were wild dogs, and then they'd run away and make us find our own way home. We were only five or six, and we didn't know our way home.

One older sibling manipulated and heightened a fear her younger sister had of being taken away from the family.

> I remember very clearly that my older sister, who is seven years older, would go to the telephone and pretend to call a man she called "Mr. Krantz." He ran an institution, she said, for "bad children," and my sister said she was going to send me there, banishing me from the family. I was terrified.

One woman, who as a child was afraid of the dark, was bullied and dominated by an older sister who preyed on that fear. Her sister wouldn't allow her the comfort and security of sleeping in the same room unless she did her sister's household chores and other tasks. The victim was caught in a bind. If she told her parents about the problem, her sister would not allow her to sleep with her and she would be alone in the dark with her fears. The victim gave in to her sister's demands and was abused as a result.

No respondents reported being emotionally abused by a sibling because of a physical handicap—aside from an inability to pronounce certain words, which may have been due to a speech defect or temporary developmental problem. However, research indicates that disabled children are high-risk candidates for physical, emotional, and sexual abuse. Their absence in this book does not mean that they aren't abused by their siblings. Instead, it could be coincidence that no handicapped people responded to the questionnaire, or it could be an indication that they learned to live with the emotional abuse by a sibling. Hopefully, the lack of handicapped respondents means parents don't tolerate abuse of siblings who have physical or mental difficulties.

Destroying Personal Possessions

Bicycles, stuffed toys, miniature trains, and clothing—they all can have special meaning and be valued possessions to a child. Everyone remembers a favorite plaything, book, or blanket from their child-hood. As adults, we may still have these objects. However, these childhood treasures can also become instruments of emotional abuse.

When siblings abuse objects, the real targets, and victims, are the children who own them. Children often invest feelings and emotions in their special toys, so harm done to the toys is actually harm done to the child who prizes them.

One woman, twenty-nine, was, as a child, very attached to a special tricycle she owned. It became the tool through which her older brother abused her.

My earliest memory of being emotionally abused occurred when I was about four years of age. My brother took apart my tricycle and hid some of the pieces so it could not be put back together. I loved my tricycle and rode it practically every day. I was so hurt by the loss of this tricycle and by my brother's sense of satisfaction that he got away with it.

A Texas respondent had similar memories of abuse from her two older brothers.

[They] called me names. I was told my parents hated me. If [my brothers] found out I cared about something—for example, toys— they were taken and destroyed in front of me.

The valued possessions of a Massachusetts survivor were also destroyed by a sibling.

My sister used to take my things and wreck them, cut my clothing up to fit her, and blackmail me to do her housework.

A woman from Maine wrote:

My brother would cut out the eyes, ears, mouth, and fingers of my dolls and hand them to me.

An adult male who was abused by an older brother reported:

A typical experience of abuse I suffered was my older brother would take whatever I had and destroy it. Then he would give it back, broken.

One small boy's Mickey Mouse ears were deliberately broken by his older brother, who laughed about it. As an adult, his memory of this remains vivid. It's reasonable to ask why an adult would care about these torn Mickey Mouse ears twenty-five years later, but the destruction of the toy is not the point. The point is that they were destroyed deliberately and with great glee. Like many other abusive siblings, this boy's brother enjoyed ruining objects that were meaningful to his victim. So, it wasn't the plastic ears that were hurt, it was the child who owned and loved them. This was not an accident, and the deliberate nature of it makes it abusive.

There is a more grown-up analogy to this point. A house is burglarized. Nothing of value is taken, and little damage is done to the property. But the victims of the burglary still feel as though someone has violated their privacy, their property, and the special meaning it has for them.

Torture or Destruction of a Pet

Although the torture or destruction of a pet may resemble the destruction of prized possessions, it involves the abuse of life—an animal's life. The emotional impact on the victim who loves, and is loved by, the animal is similar to that of victims who have objects destroyed by their siblings.

Respondents reported the torture and destruction of their pets by a sibling as an emotional abuse. A woman from Tennessee's worst and earliest experience of abuse was at the hands of an older brother a quarter of a century ago.

> My second-oldest brother shot my little dog that I loved dearly. It loved me—only me. I cried by its grave for several days. Twenty years passed before I could care for another dog.

The torture of another woman's pet was accompanied by other forms of emotional abuse.

> My older brother would come to my room and tear up my toys. He would beat my dog after tying his legs together and wrapping a cloth around its mouth to tie it shut. My brother would tell me I was stupid and would say, "Why me, why me? Why did I get a sister so stupid and dumb?" My brother also would tell me he hated me and wished I was dead.

A man, thirty-seven years old, remembers his older brother's abuse.

> He took my pet frog and stabbed it to death in front of me while I begged him not to. Then he just laughed!

The above instances of emotional abuse, whether direct or indirectly manipulative, caused real pain in victims, who responded in various ways.

How Survivors Respond

Survivors respond to emotional abuse in the same ways that they do to physical abuse. They protect themselves, scream and cry, hide from their abusers, abuse a younger sibling, and tell their parents. They may also accept and believe the abusive message, or they may fight back. Parents and professionals should watch for these responses and other clues that emotional abuse by a sibling is occurring.

Hiding

Victims of emotional abuse typically try to hide or separate themselves from their abusers. When abusers are away, victims are safe from further torment. A respondent from Texas wrote:

> I would go off by myself and daydream, write poetry, read, go and explore my mind.

A Kansas woman handled matters this way:

> I learned very early how to anesthetize myself from reality. I built a wall of bricks around myself for protection. I was laughing on the outside but absolutely dying and crying out for affection on the inside.

These coping mechanisms protect children from the emotional abuse of a sibling, but they also may have an unexpected and lingering side effect. For many survivors, the distancing techniques they relied on as children have carried over into their adult lives. This, in turn, creates other problems for survivors, which are discussed in chapter 7.

Crying

Children often cry when ridiculed or called mean names. Crying is, literally, a cry for help. But, frequently, parents don't intervene or shield their children from abuse. In these cases, crying has become the sound of helplessness, hurt, and frustration. It is less a cry for help than a plea for someone—anyone—to understand their emotional agony.

Parents often ignore crying children with the excuse that teasing is typical, or that victims did something to deserve it. Children who are ridiculed and degraded have only their parents to protect them. When their parents refuse to guard them, children have no one else in their corner.

Abusing Another Sibling

Some people reported that in response to being abused by a sibling, they turned around and abused another, even weaker sibling. A survivor of his older brother's abuse described how this happened in his family:

> I would turn it [the abuse] around on my sister. I would make her cry and go into hysterics. She would just go crazy. The more I got from my older brother, the more and more I would give my sister.

It is this kind of scenario that makes parents believe that it's normal for children to emotionally abuse one another. Parents may decide that since all their offspring behave the same way, it must be standard. Some people even reported that their parents joined in the abusive behavior by calling them names or making fun of them alongside their siblings. The extent of pain and trauma created by this kind of behavior cannot be overestimated.

Fighting Back

Unlike victims of physical abuse, who are usually not physically strong enough to fight back, victims of emotional abuse can enter into the fray. They may abuse their abusers with names, ridicule, and degradation.

A California respondent reacted to her brother's abusive teasing, name-calling, and taunting, by fighting back.

> Often I became so mad that I would hit him, but with him being four years older and much larger, he would hit me back twice as hard. I would then end up crying, feeling totally humiliated.

A Pennsylvania woman wrote that her older sister would "yell swear words and names." At first, she was shocked by her sister's language but soon "gave as good as I got, swearwordwise." Another respondent noted, "I retaliated with equally mean words." However, it is possible that fighting back has created long-term problems for adults who were abused as children. This is supported by several people who seem to relate to other adults as if they were still in combat with their siblings. Yet fighting back also has a healthy aspect to it. Survivors learn to be confident enough to stand up for themselves.

Believing the Abusive Message

One response, unique to victims of emotional abuse, is to accept, or internalize, the abusive messages they hear. That is, victims believe the names they are called and the ridicule and degrading comments directed at them. Sadly, by internalizing these messages, the abuse becomes a self-fulfilling prophesy for its victims. A survivor from Washington wrote:

> I believed everything my sister ever told me. I was dumb, homely, stupid, fat. No one would ever love me.

At forty-one, this reasonably bright adult woman still believes most of her sister's comments—that she is no good, dumb, and ugly. She still feels that her worth as a person is measured by what she does. As she describes it, her adult life consists of trying to prove that she is worth something.

How Emotional, Physical, and Sexual Abuse Interact

Only 11 of the 150 people who answered the questionnaire said that they had *only* been emotionally abused. Although all three types of sibling abuse—physical, emotional, and sexual—were treated separately on the questionnaire, most people indicated that they were abused in multiple ways. The only other exception to this were a few survivors who indicated only one type of abuse. Generally, several types of abuse work together in concert. For instance, 107 people said they had been emotionally, physically, and sexually abused. When added to the 11 people who were only emotionally abused, a total of 118 people, or 78 percent of the respondents, were emotionally abused. This is probably the most common type of sibling abuse, and among the most destructive.

Research shows that emotional abuse is a large part of all types of child abuse. It can have damaging long-term effects on self-esteem, adult relationships, and life in general.

Emotional and physical abuse interacted in the childhood of a woman abused by an older brother.

I can't remember a time when my brother didn't taunt me, usually trying to get me to respond so he would be justified in hitting me. Usually he would be saying I was a crybaby or a sissy or stupid or ugly and that no one would like me, want to be around me, or whatever. Sometimes he would accuse me of doing something, and if I denied it, he would call me a liar. I usually felt overwhelmingly helpless because nothing I said or did would stop him. If no one else was around, he would start beating on me, after which he would stop and go away. I felt helpless to stop any of it.

A survivor from an eastern state noted:

It's impossible to separate the emotional abuse from the physical abuse. I put this questionnaire aside for a week trying to think about how to separate them. I can't. I remember my older sister saying mean things to me all my life. . . . She would call me names and tell me I was in trouble, then go to my parents to complain and I would be in trouble.

A Massachusetts respondent had the same perspective.

It's impossible to separate out the physical and emotional abuse for me. In particular, it was emotionally abusive to be waiting for the physical abuse to start again.

Many people also noted how emotional and sexual abuse worked together. In the case of a New Jersey woman, her brother, nine years older, combined one with the other.

> The emotional abuse stemmed directly from the sexual abuse. The earliest memory was when I was about five years old. It's difficult for me to be specific about a single event since it's hard for me to remember many instances. I've blocked a lot out of my mind. But I always remember being afraid of being rejected by my parents. My brother was the oldest, and he made me believe that my parents would always believe him over me since I was only five and he was thirteen. So, you see, he always had some sort of power over me emotionally and physically. As a child and adolescent, I was introverted and never really shared my inner feelings with anyone. I felt like dirt and that my needs, concerns, and opinions never mattered, only those of other people. I was always in fear of both forms of abuse [emotional and sexual]. I learned to prepare myself for both. I'm so resentful that I had to do this to survive mentally in my home. My brother would always present himself in these situations as being perfect—mature, responsible, brave—a model brother. Then I'd feel like an immature, not-credible child. He'd say things like how my parents thought he was so special, being the oldest. And that if I told on him, I would destroy the entire family; my parents would divorce; I would be sent to a foster home. He had such emotional control over me in that sense that I "obeyed" him and never told. He had control over my self-image and over my body.

Although emotional abuse is held apart from physical and sexual abuse in this research, in truth it is difficult to separate them. The wounds from a physical assault may heal rather quickly, and physically there may be little or no damage when brothers rape or molest their sisters; but the final impact of any kind of abuse is on children's mental health. And that effect can stay with them the rest of their lives.

4

Sexual Abuse

Faced with the topic of sexual abuse, most parents are sure "it would never happen in my family," and "it only happens in certain kinds of families." Research data, however, tells a different story. Several surveys that focused on the backgrounds of sexually abused children showed that "[it] is prevalent in remarkable large quantity in individuals from virtually all social and family circumstances." Still other research indicates that sibling sex abusers are worse than other sex offenders, whose victims may be inside or outside the family. Sibling sex abusers commit more sex crimes for more years and often practice intrusive sexual behavior like vaginal penetration. Horribly, most sibling sexual abuse takes place when the household is asleep, or when older brothers are baby-sitting their younger siblings. Away from the watchful eyes of parents, anything can happen. And, because the victims are always within reach of their siblings, these crimes are long-term. The secrecy surrounding sibling sexual abuse ensures it is not quickly reported.

The word *incest* refers to sexual relations between people who are related, by blood, to one another. However, it is generally used to describe father–daughter relationships. Fathers who sexually abuse their daughters have received a lot of media and professional attention in recent years, but there has been little written on the frequency of sibling incest.

In the questionnaire, sibling sexual abuse was defined as inappropriate sexual contact such as unwanted touching, fondling, indecent exposure, attempted penetration, intercourse, rape, or oral or anal sex between siblings.

The Frequency of Sibling Sexual Abuse

Research shows that adults—especially those who know their victims well—are usually the perpetrators of child sexual abuse. There is evidence, however, that brother–sister sexual relationships may be five times as common as father–daughter incest. While it's difficult to determine how often children are sexually abused by adults, it's even harder to judge how often they are sexual victims of siblings because society fails to recognize the problem. Still, experts estimate that 35 percent of all females have been sexually abused; their abusers are generally male and may include siblings.

A survey of 796 undergraduates of six New England colleges found that 15 percent of the females and 10 percent of the males reported having some kind of sexual experience with a sibling— usually fondling or genital touching. Twenty-five percent of these instances involved force and occurred when the abusers were a great deal older than their sibling victims. Forty percent of the students were less than eight years old when sexually abused; but in 73 percent of cases, at least one sibling was more than eight; and in 35 percent of cases, one sibling was more than twelve.

In a study of 930 adult women living in San Francisco, 152 of them, or 16 percent, reported at least one experience of incest— father, brother, or other blood relation—by the time they were eighteen. These women had a total of 187 experiences with different abusers who were related to them. Thirty-one percent reported being sexually abused by a nonrelative before age eighteen. When these categories are combined, 357 women, or 38 percent, were sexually abused before they were eighteen, and 258, or 28 percent, had at least one such experience before age fourteen.

As terrible as these numbers are, they probably grossly underestimate the frequency of sibling sexual abuse. Embarrassment, shame, and guilt prevent both abusers and victims from discussing it, and many adults have blocked out these events of their childhood and no longer remember them. The existing information on sibling sexual abuse is usually found in reports filed in court, but these cases represent the smallest tip of the iceberg since most such abuse goes unreported and undetected.

Researchers have found that children seem to be most vulnerable to sexual abuse from an adult between the ages of six and seven, and ten and twelve. But, in truth, children are vulnerable at all ages, and the sibling sexual abuse reported in this study took place from infancy to adulthood.

Most sexual abuse of children by adults is never reported. The cases that do come to the attention of the courts, mental health clinics, and support groups are probably the exception rather than the rule. Judging from answers to the questionnaire, this is also true of victims of sibling sexual abuse.

Sexual abuse may be even more common than emotional and physical abuse. Of the 150 questionnaire respondents, 100 people, or 67 percent, were sexually abused by a sibling. Fifty people, or 37 percent, had been physically and/or emotionally abused. However, victims of sexual abuse may seek treatment more often than victims of physical or emotional abuse, and that may be the reason why more sexually abused people responded to the study. Society recognizes that sex between siblings is wrong, whereas it finds physical and emotional abuse between siblings a less clear issue. The mixed messages surrounding physical and emotional abuse may make it difficult for victims to be certain they were abused, and that in turn may make them less willing to ask for help.

Sexual abuse generally does not occur by itself. The mixing of sexual and physical abuse can be seen in the survivors' comments. Some of them were threatened with harm, and even death, if they told their parents they were being sexually abused. The mixing of sexual and emotional abuse is shown in the words of a Kansas woman, whose ten-year-older brother began raping her when she was three or four years old:

> Later, when I was about seven or eight years old, he would tease me by asking me if I was a virgin and laughing at me when I said no. It was humiliating.

While 134, or 89 percent, of the sexually abused victims in this study were women, men are also sexually abused. Other research has found much higher percentages of men who were sexually abused as children. One study revealed that while most victims were abused within the family, boys were more likely to be abused by an outsider. Professionals also believe that sexual abuse of boys is under-reported because they may be afraid of being labeled homosexuals or being seen as less "manly" because of their experiences.

Sexual Abuse and the Earliest Memories

Many survivors first remember being sexually abused when they were five to seven years old. The most frequently reported age was five, but that may simply be the earliest that survivors can remember it. Sexual abuse may have begun at a much earlier age, and some respondents said they were aware of having been abused as babies and toddlers. One woman even wrote:

> Sexual abuse was a part of my life from the time I was an infant. The age of three months is the earliest memory I have.

Many parents believe that children are not interested in, or knowledgeable about sex at age four or five, and that they only begin their sexual activity at adolescence. But even though children are not sexually mature and don't show any interest in sex, that does not mean they are not victims of sexual abuse.

To prevent sexual abuse—by a sibling or anyone else—children need to know they can say no to "secret touches" at a very early age (for more information, see chapter 9).

In most of the cases described in this book, the abusive siblings were three to ten years older than their victims. Young children may become victims simply because they don't know how to prevent their abuse.

It also is true that "you're never too old to be a victim." Several people were sexually abused through their teen and early adult years. One woman who had been frequently abused while at home believed the abuse would stop when her brother went away to college. But, one weekend she visited his school, and he attempted to rape her in the dormitory. Another respondent's older brother tried to rape her when she was married and had several children of her own. These abusers continued to view their sisters as sexual objects even into adulthood.

How does sibling sexual abuse begin and why does it continue? Had the children known how to say no to their abusers, or had the confidence that their parents would help them, much of the abuse could have been avoided. This is not to blame the victim—children must be taught how to prevent sexual abuse, even from members of their own families.

The Youngest Victims

Whenever possible, the following accounts of sexual abuse are grouped by particular situations and the victim's age. A Michigan woman wrote:

> I was three years old and I remember my oldest brother being in bed with me and rubbing against me in a way that I knew he shouldn't.

A California respondent had a story with a tragic ending.

> About age three, my older brother started fondling me, which progressed to full sexual intercourse over the next years, starting when I was about nine or ten and continuing to age fifteen, when I ran away and became a hooker.

A Maryland woman remembered:

> I was four years old and he [my older brother] told me that he wanted to show me something that Mom and Dad did. I refused. Then he offered to pay me a quarter and said that I would like it. If I turned him down, it was clear that he would hurt me. So I gave in and he made me perform oral sex with him.

Another survivor of sexual abuse from an older brother recalled:

> At approximately age four, my older brother made me take my clothes off and get into his toy box, where he fondled me and pretended to take pictures with a play camera.

The trauma of being abused has made it hard for many survivors to remember what happened. One woman, who thinks she was abused at age four, has difficulty remembering the exact time.

> It's difficult to pinpoint the first time or close to it that the sexual abuse occurred. After being in therapy, I still cannot remember. The earliest possibly was when I was four. It could have been earlier. It was mainly my brother making me touch his erection through his underwear and he touching my vagina in my underpants.

A mother from Ohio, thirty-four years old, wrote:

> My brother sat on his lower bunk and made me suck his penis. He urinated in my mouth. I was in kindergarten; he must have been in

fourth grade then. I remember I became very angry. He laughed. It seems my parents were not at home at this time or in another part of the house.

Another Ohio woman, also sexually abused at an early age, had symptoms that should have been recognized and used as a clue in detecting sexual abuse.

I was sexually abused at the age of five. I remember experiencing vaginal bleeding, but I have no memory of what happened.

A Washington respondent, who was abused three to five times a week, described her first sexually abusive encounter:

When I was five years old, my older brother—then twelve or thirteen—took me out into the woods by our house and pulled my pants down and looked at me. I don't remember if he touched me or not. The next day or so, he did it again and touched me.

Sexual abuse is often joined by threats of violence, as in the case of this woman:

I was seven, and my eldest brother took me into the woods while my mother was working. He then wanted to "play dirty" with me. He touched me on my nipples, then touched me on my vagina. He then made me touch his penis. After it was all over he said, "If you tell anyone, I will kill you!" I believed him and was frightened, and yet I didn't even realize what he was doing. To me it was like brushing my hair.

One young man, thirteen years older than his sister, threatened her in particularly vivid ways.

My brother threatened to kill me if I told our parents about him molesting me. I was three or four years of age at the time; he was about eighteen. He showed me the butcher block we kept in the cellar with the ax and blood. He said he'd kill me there if I told.

Several survivors suffered doubly when they were blamed for being abused in the first place.

I was about eight years old. My mother and stepfather had gone out for a few hours and my brother told me he wanted to imitate something he had seen between adults. He took my skirt off and was kissing and fondling me. He then laid on top of me and was rubbing himself against me, mimicking intercourse. This went on for about an hour until my mother came home and caught us. As was the usual case in my home, she didn't say anything to my brother and pinned all the blame on me for what happened.

Another respondent who was sexually abused by his two older brothers was also blamed.

About age four or five, my older brother performed oral sex on me, made me available to his older peers, and threatened me with physical violence if I told my parents. He showed me pornographic pictures, invited little girls over, and forced me into sexual play. I felt I had absolutely no control. I felt I was inferior, bad, and that there was something very wrong with me. I doubted I would be able to have a normal sex life and had fears about homosexuality and of becoming insane. Fortunately, at age thirteen my grandmother found out about the molestation, and she rescued me and became my legal guardian. My parents were happy to relinquish me because they felt I was weird and had initiated these sex acts.

Pornography also played a role in the sexual abuse of a young girl by her teenage brother.

I was nine and my brother was sixteen. I remember him showing me pictures from magazines like *Playboy, Oui, Screw,* etc., and rubbing my back. I can't remember what happened next. I just know after that it went on for two years. I was felt all over my body. I looked at lots of pictures. I was instructed on what felt good for my brother. The first time I ever saw him ejaculate, I almost vomited.

Trickery

An Indiana woman described her first sexually abusive incident:

When I was about nine, my brothers and I and some of their friends were watching TV. My brother was under a blanket on the floor, and he invited me and a friend to join him. When I did, he fondled my genitals. Then he went over to his friends on the couch and bragged about what he had done.

Trickery was often used in the encounters described in this research. An Alabama victim recalls:

I was about six years old. My brother persuaded me to lie down on the bathroom floor. There were some neighbor boys in the house. He promised not to let them in. He got me on the floor with my pants down and then opened the door. He laughed about it.

A Colorado woman in her forties was fooled under the guise of being informed about sex.

I was six or seven and my parents were at work. My brother, age eleven or twelve, persuaded me to stay home from school and smoke cigarettes. He talked to me about other secrets from parents and introduced me to sex.

Another woman wrote:

About age ten my brother approached me to engage in "research" with him. He told me he was studying breast-feeding in school and needed to see mine. He proceeded to undress me and fondle my breasts.

Still another woman explained:

I was about six to eight years old. My oldest brother called me to come up the street to his best friend's house. They told me they had a new game to play. They told me to pull my pants down, and then they told me to lie down under a table that was covered with a sheet so no one could see. Then they took turns rubbing their penises all over my lower body. I don't remember if there was penetration. They told me not to tell. I said okay.

This same woman described her reaction to what happened:

I don't remember much about it. I did not tell anyone. I remember a vague feeling of my brother [being] more important than me and I should keep quiet and do what he wants.

This victim, now the mother of a three-year-old daughter, has taught her the difference between good and secret touches.

Baby-Sitting

A Kentucky woman was abused by her older brother who was baby-sitting for her. Sibling baby-sitters can easily take advantage of the authority given them by their parents to abuse a younger sibling physically, emotionally, or sexually.

> My oldest brother was baby-sitting me and my other brother, who was outside one day after school. The abuser told me to come there to a bed in the living room—we were crowded up where we lived. He told me lie down. I was taught to do as people told me. I lay down, and he raised my dress, lowered my panties, and put his fingers on my genitals. Then he spat on me there and exposed his penis, which he then put on me down there too. I remember a white sticky stuff and a smell and slimy feel, but I don't remember any emotions at the time. When he finished, he pulled my pants up and lowered my dress. I was six years old. He was twelve the first time this happened. My mother was seldom gone, but she was gone that day.

Physical, emotional, and sexual abuse were impossible to separate in the case of a Texan who was sexually abused as a child.

> I know there was abuse before this, but I can only remember pieces of it. This is the first one where I can remember a lot of it. I am five years old. My brothers and I and two other boys were there. My brothers sold me to the two boys, and they sexually abused me. When the oldest brother forced me to touch him and put his penis in my mouth, I got sick. This made him mad. He hit me and put his pocket knife at my throat and sexually abused me. Then the other brother repeated the same acts as the oldest brother. They both urinated on me and locked me under the house, where I was tied to a pole with no clothes on. They let me out before my parents arrived. This is all I can remember.

A young woman was first sexually abused by her brother who was fourteen or fifteen at the time.

> I believe the first time was when I was six years old. He was baby-sitting me because the rest of my family was out somewhere. He came to my aunt's to pick me up, and he walked me home. I knew something felt different. He was holding my hand in a protective sort of way. It

felt nice to have my brother taking care of me. We got home, and he showed me his penis and wanted me to touch it. After that I don't remember much, except he started masturbating, and he ejaculated into the trash can. I was scared because I didn't know what was happening to him.

Many people reported that they were sexually abused while in the care of their siblings. One woman wrote about her older brother:

He was baby-sitting for me and our younger sister. She was in the tub. We were watching TV. He offered me money. He did oral sex on me.

An adult male who was sexually abused by his older brother three or four times a week recalled:

I don't remember when it began, but it started with me giving him oral sex. I usually masturbated him. I remember this happening on Sunday mornings because Mom and Dad would be gone to Grandma's.

Generally, children were sexually abused more than once, but one woman remembered a single incident that continues to enrage her. She feels her adult sexuality and her marriage were affected by this event.

There was only one instance of sexual abuse. I was eleven years old. The upstairs in our house had two bedrooms and one bath. Both he [older brother] and I always slept late on Saturday mornings. One Saturday morning I woke up but did not open my eyes because he was unbuttoning my pajamas. He was very careful, as if he were trying not to wake me. I feigned sleep. He attempted to lie on me and penetrate me. I rolled over as if stirring to avoid this. He left the room. That morning when we were alone preparing breakfast, he didn't mention anything. I told him I had had this strange dream. He smirked at me. We said no more about it. Later I received a note from him. He wanted us to share the bathroom together when we showered. I wrote back no to this.

Shortly after this incident, the girl's parents moved her to a downstairs bedroom and put her two younger brothers in the room she had been using.

One woman from Kansas wrote that it was very "painful to dig out of my repressed childhood" memories of sexual abuse. She felt that her older brother, who perpetrated the abuse, was the favored child in her family—the "golden-haired" boy:

> I was ten or eleven, in fifth or sixth grade. My parents were out of the house. My brother came into the bedroom saying, "Do you want to feel something good?" Remember, this guy was God around the house, and here he was paying attention to me. So we went to bed. I remember it hurt. I was a virgin, and he said it wouldn't hurt for long. He climaxed, and I was left hurting physically and mentally.

Another survivor recalled her first sexually abusive encounter:

> I was eleven and was taking a bath. My brother came in and forced his way into the tub and sexually assaulted me.

Abusers frequently used violence to force their victims to go along with their wishes. An Ohio woman had reason to believe the threats her brother made to her.

> I was about twelve years old. My brother told me if I didn't take my clothes off, he would take his baseball bat and hit me in the head and I would die. I knew he would do it because he had already put me in the hospital. Then he raped me.

A woman from Arizona who has been in counseling for several years described her first memory of sexual abuse—abuse that continued throughout her teenage years.

> My stepbrother and I were just goofing around in our den. He grabbed me from behind between my legs. He kept his hand there longer than necessary for our game and rubbed my clitoris through my pants. I was thirteen and he was about fifteen.

Another Arizona victim was first abused when she and her brother, a year older, shared a room while on a family vacation. The sexual encounters continued when they returned home—her brother would come into her room at night while their parents were asleep:

> My earliest memory is of my brother sneaking into my bed while we were on vacation and sharing one bedroom. This happened while my parents were still out on the town. I pretended to be asleep, and it was very difficult to determine what to do about it because of the physical pleasure but inappropriate and selfish behavior on his part.

In a single, brief sentence, a woman told the story of her first episode of sexual abuse:

I was fourteen—my brother pushed me down and raped me.

A woman of forty-two described the feelings she had when first abused by her brother. Her brief but poignant statement expresses the feelings of so many victims of sibling sexual abuse:

I remember waking up as my brother was touching me. I was so scared!

Sexual Abuse: What Usually Happens

Again, only a few people responding to the questionnaire had been sexually abused only once. For most victims, their abuse continues and they cannot escape from it. It increases in intensity, and often is joined by physical and emotional abuse. This ongoing trauma is also suffered by victims of father–daughter incest, and only ends when the child is old enough to physically stop the assault, or it is discovered and appropriately ended.

One respondent wrote:

I can't remember exactly how the sexual abuse started, but when I was smaller, there was a lot of experimenting. He would do things to me like putting his finger in my vagina. Then as I got older, he would perform oral sex on me.

Another woman recalled:

Initially I was forced to masturbate him one night, but from then on it moved quickly to oral sex on him and eventually rape.

The word *rape* needs a clear definition here. In most states, rape is legally defined as the penetration of the penis into the vagina under force or the threat of force. Based on a growing understanding of sexual abuse and its effects on victims, rape is now being used more broadly. Rape can now be used to mean any sexual activity in which force, threats of force, or threats in general are used. An example of the latter would be when an older brother tells his sister not to "tell" or he would be sent to jail and their parents would divorce.

This broadening of the term "rape" is important both for how "rapists" are prosecuted and for how victims are treated. When abusers use real or threatened violence, it brings their action into the realm of rape, whether or not penetration has occurred. For example, fondling a victim's genitals can no longer be thought of as less harmful than sexual intercourse because in both cases the victim's privacy has been abused through an aggressive act. In other words, the victim has been raped. By definition, a victim of sexual abuse is a victim of an aggressive act. The woman quoted above had, legally, been raped—she had sexual intercourse under the threat of force. But, in fact, she had been raped many times before when she had been forced to masturbate and perform oral sex on her brother against her wishes.

After the first episode of sexual abuse, how did it continue? One woman from Idaho wrote:

It began as games and grew to "look and feel." As I became older, he played with my breasts and then fondled my genitals, always wanting but never achieving intercourse. He showed me with his fingers how it would feel.

One boy approached his younger sister saying that his sexual abuse was an "experiment."

He made it into an experiment. He would have me undress, and he would look and touch me—especially my vagina. I was frequently required to touch him on his penis. He would have me in the playhouse or basement room. At age nine or ten, he started penetrating me—again, as an experiment. No emotions or feeling. I was told not to tell because it was an experiment and if I told it would fail. There was more to his convoluted logic, but that was the gist of it.

Another survivor said the abuse occurred whenever her parents went out—at least once a week. After the first time, the abuse progressed.

It became much more frequent as he got older. It mostly happened when I was in sixth to ninth grade, ages eleven to fifteen. I knew he would try, so I would lock myself in my room. He would pick the lock and force me to the ground or bed. I can remember yelling at him, or crying, or begging, or throwing myself down and saying "Go ahead," which he did, or saying I would tell. His response was, "Well, if you're going to tell, I might as well go ahead." I tried everything I could think of—for example, appealing to his morals as a brother. One time I remember holding a knife to myself. He got it away, always laughing. He'd force off my clothes, rub and suck my breasts, put his penis between them, and rub. He would perform oral sex on me often. I remember sucking his penis once. He did not come in my mouth. He would rub his penis all over my vulva and press against my vagina. He never inserted it, just pressed against it. . . . I kept a calendar during his senior year of high school. I had made it a "countdown" of when he'd move out upon graduation, with the numbers going down.

Sibling sexual abuse does not happen just in poor or uneducated families. The respondent quoted above had a father who completed graduate school and a mother who finished several years of college. Religious families are also not immune to such abuse, as another survivor explained:

When it all started, usually both of my brothers approached me together, often while my parents were away in the evenings and they were left to baby-sit. They would drag me kicking and screaming up the stairs and usually lay me on the floor and pull my clothes off. They took turns fondling me and having me masturbate them. During all of this, they would make crude comments about my body. Sometimes they would ejaculate all over me. My father was a minister, and my parents were often gone in the evening, so there was plenty of time for all this to happen. As the years went by, I became much more compliant and went with them when they approached me. It also became a matter of usually one or the other approaching me at a time.

A Kansas woman described the progression of her sexual abuse:

He [older brother] started the activity by fondling me and progressed to having me manually stimulate his penis. After the initial two incidents, I refused to cooperate further. He then began to expose himself to me when we were alone and try to force me to participate. My refusal led to a stage of terrorism, where he would chase me and threaten me.

A common tactic for abusers was to isolate their victims so that they could take advantage of them. One woman explained how her brother would know when to attack her.

He would always seem to know when I was alone and when no one could hear. I would always know when he entered a room when it would happen. He would make me terrified. I would think, "Oh, no, not again!" He'd try to compliment me in a sexual way. Complimenting a four- to six-year-old on her "great breasts" was not what I'd call a turn-on. He'd either undress me or make me undress myself. He would undress and make me touch his erection. I hated that because he'd force me to do it and would hold my hand against it to almost masturbate him. He never orgasmed, though. He'd touch me, almost like he was examining me. A few times he had oral sex on me. . . . He attempted intercourse, but that was difficult. He'd force my legs apart, and I was always so scared that my muscles were so tight and my opening was so small, he never really could enter without severe pain. I would say he was hurting me, which he was, and I'd cry in hopes he'd stop. Sometimes he did. Other times he would force himself inside of me so that I would hurt for days.

Similarly, a woman from Michigan said:

One thing my brother always did was to isolate his victim. He was always saying "Come over here. I want to show you something," or "Come on, let's go for a ride."

Sexual abuse of victims also continues at night, when other family members are sleeping. As one woman remembered:

I would try to put off going to bed. I would try to cover up tight with my blankets. It didn't help. My brother would come into my room and touch me all over. I would pretend I was asleep. After he left, I would cry and cry.

When sexual abuse occurs at night, victims often "defend" themselves by pretending to be asleep. Being physically and emotionally powerless in these instances, victims may use sleeping as a psychological roadblock against their pain and suffering. It seems akin to saying, "If I'm asleep, I won't be aware of what is happening and it won't hurt me as much."

Two survivors wrote:

My brother would come into my room at night and fondle my breasts and genitals. He used to put his fingers inside me and would put his penis between my legs. He never tried to penetrate me with his penis. I always pretended to be asleep.

Typically, my brother would sneak into my bed in the middle of the night and "experiment" on me. I would stir and try to scare him away by pretending to wake up, but he was undaunted. He would wait until I seemingly fell back to sleep and start again—vaginal penetration or oral sex.

One respondent's sexual abuse began when she was three or four years old. Her brother, thirteen years older, forced her to perform oral sex on him, wrenching back her head with his hand in her hair.

I had already learned that if I cried out in pain he would beat me worse, so I had to remain silent until he left. The abuse continued through the years—sometimes in his car, sometimes in my room at night. I was terrified of him. I was terrified to go to my room at night. I wedged myself on the cold linoleum floor (cold Connecticut winters) between my bed and the wall, trying to hide from him at night and stay awake so the nightmares wouldn't come. It was the family joke that I must keep falling out of my bed at night.

While most of the survivors in this research are women, a few are men. These are the comments of a man who was sexually abused by his brother:

My brother caught me masturbating once. That's when the sexual abuse began. At night he would have me fondle him, masturbate him, and fellate him, depending on what he wanted. He threatened to tell Mom about catching me masturbating if I didn't go along. The abuse went on about a year or two. It was always at night. He would lie on his back. A street light would shine across his body through the curtains, and he would call me to come "do" him. I felt as if I were on stage with the street light and trapped in a bad part. I hated him immensely. Finally, after a year or so I told him he could tell whomever he wanted, but I wouldn't do it anymore. The abuse stopped, but the damage was done. My feelings would haunt me into high school, college, and my marriage.

In the same way that victims were physically intimidated during their periods of sexual abuse, they were also emotionally threatened and sometimes made to believe that it was their own fault. Comments from three survivors show how these various abuses worked in concert:

It usually started with him [my brother] yelling at me. Then he would hurt me somehow—cut me, hit me, etc. Then he would overpower me to rape me. After this, he always told me this was my fault.

I would be in my bed asleep. He would jump in the bed with me. I would try and push him out. I was just not strong enough, and he would always keep that baseball bat and knife with him.

He would lay me down and put his big fist in my face, and he would say, "If you scream, this is what you'll get." Then he would sexually abuse me.

Victims wanted—and sometimes attempted—to stop the abuse, but were helpless to do so. An Arizona woman's comments depict this:

The sexual abuse was on a daily basis. I think my brother enjoyed it, and it became a regular habit. I would say no, but my pleas never helped. I felt sorry not only for him but also for myself.

Equally, another woman:

He [her brother] would sneak into my room at night and put his hand down my pajama bottoms and rub my clitoris until I had an orgasm. Then he would leave. I was too scared to move and wasn't sure what was happening. My parents were usually out playing bridge when this occurred. As it progressed, however, sometimes he would sneak into my room when everyone was asleep. I locked my door, but he slit the screens and got in through the window.

While most of the incidents of sexual abuse consisted of masturbation, oral sex, or intercourse, some other people were victims of inappropriate touching and sexually slanted remarks. Several survivors describe this sort of abuse:

My brother, two years older, would commonly grab my chest where my breasts were developing and would twist. When I would ask him to stop, he would say, "You love it and you know it."

When I was in my teens, my brother would say provocative things to me to see how I'd respond.

My brother would come up behind me and grab my breasts. He would verbally harass me and constantly make sexual references, even when we were older teenagers.

The feelings of the survivors as they recall their years of sexual abuse are best expressed by these comments:

It's too much to even put into words on paper.

I still feel so hurt and sad for that poor little defenseless girl. They raped her—she suffers still.

The latter comment suggests a problem often associated with sexual abuse of a child—multiple personality. Victims handle the abuse by denying that it really happened to them. Instead, they push the trauma into a different part of their personality and believe it occurred in someone else's life. The development of multiple personalities thus becomes a way to survive the severe shock of sexual abuse and the feelings resulting from it.

The Victims Respond

Children respond to sexual abuse differently than they respond to emotional and physical abuse. Most children react in kind to emotional abuse—fighting back verbally, ridiculing, and calling their siblings names. Generally, this doesn't work very well, as their siblings either intensify the abuse or shift over to other, more physical tactics.

Victims of physical abuse—who are usually smaller and weaker than their abusers—are often unable to fight back. Thus, they tend to hide and withdraw into themselves to get away from their abusers.

But in cases of sexual abuse, most children don't fight back. When children do fight back, they demonstrate their right and their ability to say no—and that, in turn, may put a halt to the abuse.

As previously noted, many children pretend to sleep during their assaults. This is also true in cases of father–daughter incest, where children who are unable to fight off their abusers "play possum." Unfortunately, in courtrooms children are frequently attacked by lawyers and discredited by juries because they did not protest or cry out during their assaults. This only adds to their guilt and self-blame. Thus, the entire sexual assault situation—from traumatic incident to the investigation that may follow it—can be psychologically devastating for any victim, particularly a child.

Another, more common response is to submit or accept the sexual abuse. Victims, especially the youngest ones, often aren't even aware of what is going on when an older brother or sister uses them in sexual play. Only afterward—sometimes even years later—do they feel shame or guilt about their actions. They often cope with such feelings by blaming themselves for going along with the abuse, even though they may have had no other choice. Considering their age, they probably don't know much about, or even how to fight off, sexual assault.

In addition, sexual abuse usually happens in a shroud of secrecy. Like adult abusers, sibling perpetrators often approach their victims as friends. They may say that what happens is to be their little secret, thus seducing the victim into going along with the abuse in silence.

Finally, sibling sexual abuse usually occurs in the context of threats. Older siblings threaten their victims with physical harm if their parents find out. Or abusers tell their victims that they'll both be punished if their parents are told. The latter tactic leaves victims feeling partly responsible for the sexual activity. Thus, victims pretend that nothing has happened, for fear of being punished either by their abusers or by their parents. As one survivor remarked:

> Once my mother was suspicious. She confronted my brothers and they denied it. She told them she would ask me. Then she waited several days. During that time, my brothers told me I'd better not tell her or they'd get me into trouble.

Some victims of sexual assault are called "accessories to sex." In these cases, abusers pressure, bribe, lie to, or take advantage of victims in order to have sex. These "accessories" end up having sex either due to circumstances or because they're not mature enough to break away from their abusers.

Even though accessories are pressured into silence, their emotional pain is very loud indeed. Survivors are forced to silently bear the anxiety, shame, guilt, and other destructive emotions by themselves. The only sign of this turmoil is that victims may withdraw and want to be alone. These sorts of behaviors should be important clues for parents, teachers, and other adults that children may have problems they are scared to discuss. These behaviors may be signs that children are trying to repress the emotions surrounding a painful experience.

A victim from Colorado repressed her sexual abuse for years, until she was pregnant.

> I had no recollection of the sexual abuse until I was pregnant with my daughter. I then started having very graphic nightmares about my brother raping me. I was about three or four years old in the dreams. He was on top of me, holding me down and forcing himself into me. I was crying and screaming at him to stop. He would say, "You know you like it." I thought I was a pervert to have those dreams, so I didn't tell anyone about them until when my daughter was about a year old. I was physically abusing her, and I went to Parents Anonymous for help. The sponsor asked me if I had been sexually abused. I said I hadn't, but I told her about the nightmares. She said she thought it had really happened. With her support and encouragement, I asked my sisters first. They said he had abused them, but there was no penetration. Then I confronted him. I told him just exactly what was in the dreams, down to the last details. There was a silence; then he said, "You are right. I did that."

It is important to understand why more sibling abusers are not "told on" and stopped. Psychiatrist Dr. Roland Summit studied the responses of sexually abused girls and came up with a theory that explains a great deal. Normally abused by their fathers or other close male relatives, these children undergo a "sexual abuse accommodation syndrome." The syndrome has five categories: secrecy; helplessness; entrapment and accommodation; delayed, unconvincing disclosure; and retraction. The first two steps—secrecy and helplessness—refer to the vulnerable position the child is in. The abuse takes place in *secrecy*, and the child is *helpless*, either physically or emotionally, to do anything about it. The next three steps refer to what happens to these children after being abused. Following the first episode of abuse, victims feel *trapped* and unable to refuse their abusers. If they *disclose* what has happened, it is usually because the abuse has continued. Even then, the disclosure is made at great emotional cost because victims may be punished by their abusers and are fearful of the effect on the family. In fact, the disclosure may not be convincing because the family doesn't want to believe the victim, and because the abuser denies the sex took place. Faced with the chaotic aftermath of disclosure, victims often *retract* and literally retreat from their accusations. While this sexual abuse accommodation syndrome was devised to explain adult–child sexual abuse, it seems to be true for sibling sexual abuse as well.

Sexual Curiosity

How is sexual curiosity different from sexual abuse? When two small siblings take a bath together, and look at or maybe even touch each other's genitals, is that abuse? Is everything that happens between siblings abuse?

Not all interactions between siblings are abusive. Although chapter 8 focuses on the difference between abusive and normal behaviors, sexual curiosity deserves a brief discussion here.

Sexual curiosity is normal. All children explore their own bodies and, to some extent, they may explore another child's body as well. This is one way that children discover sexual differences or check out what their parents told them about boys and girls. Two small children touching each other's bodies does not leave them fated to a life of emotional chaos and suffering.

For example, a nursery school attendant sees four-year-old Tim showing his penis to five-year-old Sue. When they realize the attendant saw what happened, Tim blames Sue, saying she told him to show her. Sue denies it. The attendant reports the activity to the teacher, who takes the children aside and explains sexuality to them in words they can understand. The teacher also reviews with them the difference between good and secret touches.

Sexual activity between consenting partners probably presents the least risk of unhappy results. But young children who consent to sex may do so because they can't anticipate the problems involved. Or they may consent simply because they don't know enough to refuse. Finally, they may consent because they passively accept what is happening to them.

Our society has a wide range of attitudes about sex. Some people are very uncomfortable with sexual issues and, instead of talking about sex to their children, pretend these issues don't exist. Others support open sexual activity in front of their children and encourage them to experiment sexually. Neither approach ensures their children will have healthy attitudes toward sex.

Because sexual abuse has such a profound impact on children, parents must take an active approach to teaching them about sexuality. Such an approach includes giving children information about sex that is right for their age and development, teaching children about good and secret touches and how to refuse them, and providing an atmosphere where children can talk about their sexual concerns.

Sexual abuse by siblings is a terrible reality. Its impact on young victims can last a lifetime. The seriousness of the problem means that parents must help their children understand about sex, including how to prevent it.

Understanding physical, emotional, and sexual abuse between siblings, which is the subject of chapter 6, also requires an understanding of how parents react to it. Parents' awareness, or lack of awareness of what's going on, and how they respond, contribute to the lasting effects of the abuse itself, as seen in the adult lives of the victims.

Parents React to Sibling Abuse

After reading these accounts of sibling abuse, it's fair to ask: Weren't the parents aware of what was going on in their own houses? How did they react? Didn't they do anything to stop it? The answers to these questions are provided in the words of the survivors.

Parental Awareness

Everyone who answered the research questionnaire was asked the following question: Were your parents aware of what was happening? It was asked three times—once each after the sections on physical, emotional, and sexual abuse.

Their responses indicate that parents were more likely to be aware of physical and emotional abuse than they were of sexual abuse. Seventy survivors of physical abuse, and eighty-one survivors of emotional abuse believed their parents were aware of it. This is understandable as the resulting cuts and bruises of physical abuse are hard to hide; and emotional abuse is often hurled by one sibling at another in front of parents. But only eighteen of the survivors of sexual abuse thought their parents knew about it. This, too, makes sense. Sexual abuse occurs when parents are away from home or sleeping.

Another reason parents were unaware of sexual abuse is because they simply weren't told. Victims often feel they can't tell them, for several reasons. First of all, victims don't always understand they are being abused. As adults, however, they see things much more clearly than they did as children. Second, since the abuse often takes place when older siblings are in charge, and victims have been told to obey them, they may believe their parents know what is going on. A third reason is that abusive siblings may threaten victims in order to make sure that parents aren't told. In these cases, victims are scared of being badly hurt by their siblings the next time they are left alone together. Fourth, victims tend to blame themselves if they get sexual pleasure from the experience. They're afraid that if they "tell," their siblings will say the victims enjoyed it. To make matters worse, abusive siblings often blame their victims for not resisting their sexual advances. Finally, victims may not report sexual abuse because the climate in the household makes it impossible to do so. One woman did the best she could to communicate it under the circumstances.

> I remember every time my parents went out, I'd sit in my parents' room while they got ready and I'd ask them, "Do you really have to go out tonight? Can't you stay home?" That's as close as I could get to telling them or asking them for their protection.

This same woman felt that she might have been able to tell her parents if they had been easier to talk to.

> Somehow they should have provided a family atmosphere in which their children—me, at this point—could have approached them with the situation without being afraid of getting into trouble.

She was uncomfortable talking with her parents about such things, and her parents did not encourage open communication. Just because parents are physically present doesn't mean that they are emotionally available. This woman's parents may have been too busy or preoccupied to listen closely to their daughter or to watch for warning signs of her abuse. This does not mean that active or working parents are more likely to have abused children. It simply means that all parents must watch and listen carefully for obvious and hidden truths.

Parents Respond

When parents are aware of sibling abuse, how do they respond to it? Do they do anything about it?

Some parents do intervene and stop the abuse. Children growing up in such homes are not the ones who responded to the research questionnaire. People whose parents took charge don't identify themselves as victims even though they may have been abused one or more times. The fact that their parents protected them and ended the problem kept the abuse from having such an impact on their lives.

Parents of the people who answered the questionnaire responded in ways that did not help. In fact, they sometimes made matters worse. Different types of responses are noted below to show why certain reactions don't work.

Ignoring or Minimizing the Abuse

One of the most common responses to sibling abuse is to ignore it or pretend it isn't as bad as victims claim. This is particularly true of physical and emotional abuse. Abusive behavior is often excused as sibling rivalry, or a gender-related ruckus. "Boys will be boys; kids will be kids," is a common refrain for many parents. While certain behaviors are normal for children, depending on their maturity, there is no excuse for abuse.

The parents of a California woman who was physically abused by her older brother did the following:

> They ignored or minimized the abuse. They told me, "Boy are boys and they need to clear their system."

This woman felt—and was—helpless. The only people who could protect her believed that abuse was a normal part of childhood.

Another woman, frequently abused by her brother, wrote that her parents excused the behavior by saying, "He doesn't know his own strength." Not only did this not help the victim, it made matters worse. In effect, her parents said she'd have to accept the abuse. No attempt seems to have been made to confront her brother about either his strength or his behavior.

A woman thirty-three years old had a similar experience with her parents:

> My mother would say that he (my brother) was not hitting me hard enough for me to complain. Or she would say that he is going through a stage and would outgrow it.

Incidentally, the "stage" he was going through included throwing his eight-year-old sister down a flight of stairs and beating her up two or three times a week.

A man thirty-seven years old physically abused by his brother also sought protection from his parents.

> I told them once, and they didn't believe me, and they would leave me alone with him again. Then I really suffered for telling on him. I soon learned not to tell.

A Canadian woman, also abused by her brother, got this reaction from her parents:

> My parents had no reaction to anything except denial. My mother may have made a token effort to stop it but she was very ineffectual.

Obviously, when parents ignore or minimize problems of physical abuse, they do not go away. If anything, abusers are given a kind of silent permission to continue because they know their parents will not get involved.

A survivor of her brother's physical abuse reported that her parents

> saw it as normal sibling rivalry and did not correct any of what he (my brother) said. If they were around [when it was occurring], they would just say we had to learn to get along better.

Another woman wrote that her parents

> dismissed it as normal sibling rivalry and said it was probably half my fault. They were unwilling to become involved.

Emotional abuse also does not end when parents ignore it. Pretending it's normal, or that it isn't too bad, also leaves victims feeling unprotected. Solutions were suggested by one woman:

> They [my parents] could have talked to my brother to help him realize how hurtful his teasing and name-calling was. If this did not work, they could have forbidden this kind of behavior and punished appropriately. Perhaps they could have been a better role model, also.

A Kansas woman described her parents' reaction to the emotional abuse in their household:

My parents seemed to think it was cute when he ridiculed me.

Another type of reaction was described by a Tennessee woman:

It wasn't abuse to them. It was normal. Our abuse to each other as siblings disturbed their own peace, and so they'd yell or get in on it, too. Then, when Mom and Dad were not watching, the big boys would get even anyway and it would be worse, so I just as soon didn't want Mom and Dad "protecting" me, or Mom and Dad getting into another fight with each other—a vicious, escalating, abusive cycle of insanity!

The parents of a Pennsylvania woman knew her brother was emotionally abusive but "framed their reaction in such a way that it seemed okay." Her parents would tell her, "The smartest one keeps quiet. All kids fight." Another victim wrote that her parents would tell her, "Sisters must love each other!" On her questionnaire, in large letters, she added the word "GREAT!" as if to say, "What good did that do me?" Her sister continued to abuse her.

"They laughed it off," was how one woman's parents responded to problems between their two girls. Similarly, an Arizona woman wrote that her parents were also amused:

Everything was always a joke to them. They laughed at my emotions. Usually their reply was to quit complaining—"You'll get over it."

One mother tolerated the emotional abuse among her children because, when she was a child, physical abuse had been normal in her family. She excused the problem because she believed the abuse was less severe than what she had received as a child.

Another woman wrote:

Both my parents minimized my brother's angry, aggressive behavior, especially my mother, who I don't think knew what to do. I received little support from my parents. I often went to my mother for her to intervene, but she made minimal efforts. I soon began to feel very powerless as a child and felt that I had to just put up with my brother's abuse.

Some parents ignored or minimized physical and emotional abuse among their children because they were abusive themselves. Their children's behavior didn't seem abnormal because it mirrored their own actions.

A California respondent wrote:

My father was so emotionally abusive to us, especially to my brother, that he probably wouldn't have noticed that there was anything wrong with the way my brother treated me. My brother in essence was doing to me what was done to him.

Similarly, the parents of an Arkansas woman

didn't do anything to stop it. They didn't talk to me to help me understand it because they emotionally abused me, too.

A New York survivor had the same experience:

My brother constantly belittled me, telling me how stupid, incompetent, ugly, useless, etc., I was. But again, he was only modeling our mother's behavior.

Three other respondents described their own emotionally abusive family structures:

My parents had no reaction to the emotional abuse I experienced. Such "put-downs" were relatively frequent on their part as well.

They (my parents) were abusive, too, so it was just part of everyday life.

My parents, especially my mother, was the greatest one to emotionally abuse the whole family. It seems my older brothers and sisters copied her.

Some parents not only excused abusive sibling behavior, they recommended it as a positive experience. "It will make you tough," a father often told his daughter after her two older brothers reduced her to tears, saying she was ugly.

Blaming the Victim

Not all parents pretended nothing wrong was happening. Some parents recognized there was a problem—so they blamed the victim for it. When parents blame victims, they become victims a second time. Worse still, abusers learn that they will not be held responsible, that abusive behavior is accepted, and that their victims somehow "deserve" to be abused. The abuse, therefore, continues.

The woman who was tickled until she vomited was told, "You must have asked for it." Her parents had similar responses when she was shoved and punched by the same sibling. Judging from answers to the questionnaire, this is a fairly common reaction. Rather than examining what happened, victims are made to feel guilty for it.

Another survivor was blamed by her parents:

I was hurt, but my sister was not blamed, or it was turned around that I had done something to cause it. She was never wrong.

One woman's parents did attempt to intervene when their children fought. They

would usually break it up, but with me being the oldest I'd always get accused of causing the problem and be told I should set a better example and I wouldn't get hurt.

As a child, one woman told her mother about being physically abused by her two brothers, five and eight years older than the victim. Now forty-two years old, she still vividly remembers her mother's response:

Mom would say, "You should know better than to be there." "You should know better, they don't."

A typical abusive situation and parental response was described by a Texas woman, thirty-three years old, abused by her older brother and sister:

It started when I was ten or eleven. My sister would hit me, and my mother would hit me because she said I deserved it if my sister hit me. I always tried to be good, but a lot of times it seemed like for no reason this would happen. It was as if my mother was giving my sister the okay to treat me as she saw fit.

A victim of her older brother's sexual abuse reported:

Most of the time the abuse was happening, I lived with my divorced mother. I'm not sure that she knew what was happening. But even if she had, I don't think she would have stopped it. Her philosophy was that you just took what men and life dished out to you and you didn't complain because you probably did something to deserve it. My mother treated all her daughters with disrespect and had none for herself, so my brother learned early on that he didn't have to respect us either. The abuse finally stopped because I ran away from home when I was sixteen and never came back.

Another survivor reported being blamed for her own abuse. Her parents

didn't know but they would have blamed me or at least made excuses for him [her brother]. My mother would say, "Men are hunters, don't trust any, not even your own brother." But she meant it in general, not for her son, the "King."

A California woman was even blamed for being sexually abused by her brother.

When I hinted that I was having problems, they placed the blame on me or they ignored it. My mother once walked in on us and beat me up. She told me I was a slut, that I deserved it.

A male victim of his older brother's sexual abuse did not tell his parents but believed he knew how they would respond:

Since I was the "good son" in the family, an excellent student, always helpful, never in trouble, I would have received all the blame and been the target of their anger. They would have said that I should have known better and that I could have stopped my brother. He would have been yelled at, but would not have received the shame that I did.

Many emotionally and even physically abusive squabbles between two siblings may, in fact, be caused by both of them. There is some truth to the old adage, "It takes two to tango." The "interactional theory" of sibling abuse argues that some children act in ways that may make them targets, or victims. This does not excuse the abusive sibling, it simply states that victims may unknowingly encourage their own problems. Analyzing the contributions of each sibling is an important part of the peaceful problem-solving techniques described at the end of this chapter.

Doubt and Disbelief

When victims of sibling abuse—especially sexual abuse—do tell their parents what's going on, they are not necessarily believed. These children are, once again, made victims a second time around. They are being abused, and their parents won't stop the abuse because they don't believe it exists. To get an inkling of how this feels, consider the following story. You are getting out of your car in the parking lot of a large shopping mall. A stranger approaches, pulls out a gun, and demands all your money. He takes your wallet and runs to a nearby car and drives off. You notice a police officer standing close by, ticketing some cars. You scream for help. The police officer looks up, sees you, and goes back to ticketing the cars. You run to the nearest store to call the police. A few minutes later, the police arrive and you describe the crime. The officer writes down a few notes on his report form while you talk. Then he says, "I really don't believe you. But if it's true, you must have done something to make that man rob you."

A New York woman felt the double blow of this treatment very clearly.

> When I tried to tell my father about it, he called my mother and brother into the room, told them my accusations, and asked my brother if it was true. Naturally, he said I was lying, and my mother stood there supporting him. Nothing happened, except that I got beaten later by my mother for daring to say anything and for "lying." My brother then knew that from then on, there was nothing he couldn't do to me. He was immune from punishment. Never again did I say a word, since to do so would only have meant more abuse from them both. I concluded it was better to keep my mouth shut.

When parents don't believe what they are told, their children may conclude that it's useless to tell them anything at all. Thus, when the abuse changes, or gets worse, parents may never find out about it. Their children, in turn, get locked into a cycle of abuse. This was the case of one young man:

> When I tried to tell them about the beatings I was taking, they didn't believe me, and they would leave me alone with him again. So when it came to the sexual abuse, I didn't think they would believe me.

Research shows that almost all mothers will believe that their children are being sexually abused if they accuse someone like a grandfather, uncle, or cousin. They are somewhat less likely to believe it if they accuse their fathers. And only about half of them believe it when the accused is a stepfather or live-in partner. Basically, mothers are less likely to believe such reports if the accused person is part of the nuclear, and not extended, family.

Research shows that the age of children reporting such abuse is also important. The younger the children, the more likely their mothers are to believe them. In fact, almost all mothers believed their children if they were two to five years old, but less than two thirds believed their children if they were twelve to seventeen years old. Perhaps this is because mothers think younger children don't know enough about sex to lie about it. Or maybe mothers don't want to see their teenage daughters as attractive "competitors" for their adult partner.

Equally, women who had been passive victims of sexual abuse as children tend not to believe their own daughters are being abused. Typically, these mothers doubt their daughters' claims, become angry with them, or, worse, blame them for being sexually abused. It seems likely that these women never resolved the problems and guilt caused by their own abuse and thus are unwilling to cope with the matter raised this time by their daughters.

It is important for parents and professionals to focus on what victims are saying, and not to place them in the terrible situation of being doubted or not believed.

Indifference

Indifference is another parental response to sibling sexual abuse. Some parents may simply not know what to do. Others may be overwhelmed with their own problems, or under so much stress they are unable to look beyond themselves.

One respondent wrote:

> I told my mother about my older brother molesting me about two years after it happened, and she asked me what I expected her to do about it. . . . I never bothered to tell her about other things that happened because obviously she didn't care.

Other Inappropriate Responses

While some parental responses are ineffective, other responses actually trigger more abuse. One woman, forty-four, was abused by her brother who was six years older—starting at age four. She used to think that her parents didn't believe her; however, as an adult looking back on what happened in her childhood, she now believes her parents simply didn't know what to do about it. Her brother started out by kicking and torturing her pet rabbit, and beating his sister, and progressed into frightening and threatening his mother. Another woman wrote that her parents would tell her three older brothers to stop physically abusing her, but the behavior would start up again after a brief lull.

Similarly, an Alaskan woman reported:

> My mom [father was dead] would tell my brother to stop abusing me—he was not allowed to hit girls. But it went in one ear and out the other. He did not listen to what she said. . . . She got tired of me asking her to do something about it. She would just give up.

This woman's mother obviously didn't know how to prevent her son's abusive behavior. Simply put, her intervention tactics were not effective.

Another inappropriate response to sibling abuse is to physically punish the abusive sibling. A young woman victimized by her older sister provides an example. Her parents

> would yell at her [my sister] and pinch and bite her to "teach" her how it felt so she'd stop doing it. It only made it worse for me, though. They'd clean my wounds and tell me a story to tell my teacher to explain my bandages and markings.

This approach might be called giving abusers "a dose of their own medicine." Some parents do this with small children—biting a toddler who has bitten them, or telling a child who has been slapped to slap back. But this type of parenting doesn't teach the child any new behavioral patterns, it just mimics—and encourages—abusive behavior.

One woman reported that when her father found out she was being physically abused by her brother, he beat the boy so badly that she resolved not to tell her father ever again. This victim blamed herself for her brother's beating, and for being the type of person her brother hated.

Just as violence can beget more violence, violent discipline can promote more brutality. Abusers may get even angrier when punished and will probably lash out again at their victims (or parents).

One survivor's account shows why abusing the abuser doesn't work:

> My older brothers received a severe beating when I told my parents how they were abusing me. The severity of the beating, however, discouraged me from ever reporting again what happened because I wanted to avoid a more violent outcome.

When reporting an abuse can trigger a chain of violent events that affects the whole family, it may discourage victims from discussing matters with their parents.

> My father would never know [about the victim's abuse from an older brother and sister] because my mother would never tell him for fear of what he would do. She would try to hide it from him. She would say, "Don't tell your father; don't get him started."

Similarly, a California woman wrote:

> On a couple of instances my father did know [about her abuse from an older brother] when I cried out in pain. Once my father beat my brother for hours about not hitting a woman. When my brother started crying, my stepmother went to comfort him. My father then hit her in the face for taking my brother's side.

Research shows that parents are more likely to punish older siblings than younger ones. This tendency usually encourages the younger children to be verbally and physically aggressive, knowing that their parents will often side with them. A more effective approach is for parents to stop the fighting, help solve the problem, and refrain from punishment.

Some parents punish all their children equally when they hear about abuse between them. This method hurts victims a second time, rather than protecting them. A Louisiana woman's parents believed in this tactic:

> If any of the siblings made me cry for some reason, and my parents became aware of it, we would all get whipped.

The father of a Montana survivor handled the fighting among his children this way:

> Dad would yell at us and threaten us with a belt if we didn't shut up. His anger was directed not at my brother, who abused me, but at all the kids. . . . I learned to cry silently because of my dad. The belt was worse than my brother's abuse.

Being inconsistent is another parenting style that doesn't help. The three brothers of an Ohio woman were sometimes beaten, sometimes yelled at, and sometimes ignored when they abused their sister. They continued to mistreat her because there was no firm, consistent message that their behavior would not be tolerated.

Another victim was told that her siblings were just jealous of her and that God would eventually reward her for being good when they were bad to her. This let her siblings know that they could continue to abuse her with impunity, at least until they were punished by God.

One respondent from Tennessee, who described her home life as a "death camp existence," believed that if her parents knew her brother was sexually abusing her,

> there would have been more beatings for everyone all around. Instead of a constant, at-random sort of violence, there would have been a concerted and pointed effort to make people even more miserable.

Children have all sorts of reasons for keeping quiet about their abuse. This seems particularly true of sexual abuse. One New York woman didn't tell her parents because she wanted to protect her mother from any emotional consequences.

> If my father had known, he probably would have beaten my brother and thrown him out of the house. My mother would have insisted that we both get counseling. She would have blamed herself. She would have thought my brother's problem stemmed from the emotional abuse he suffered from my father as an alcoholic.

Joining In—The Worst Response

Perhaps the saddest thing of all is when parents join one child in abusing another. When victims are abused by the very people whom they need to protect them, it can be disastrous. There is no one else for victims to rely on. The terrible unhappiness they feel is understandable.

An Ohio woman, already abused by her older sister, felt even worse when

my mother would pick up on it and also make fun of me.

A respondent from Arizona wrote:

When I was six and started school, the girls took me in the bathroom and put me in the toilet to wash me. Then they called me "stinkweed." I was crushed. When I got home, I talked about it. Even my whole family laughed at me and called me that daily. It still hurts. It's something I'll never forget. They still remind me of it.

When he saw his daughter protecting herself from her brother's assaults, one father thought they were fighting, so, "Dad would join in and hit us harder."

Once parents are made aware of what's going on, they will react or respond in some way. Even no reaction is a kind of responding. But responses like the above are always wrong.

The Right Responses

What is the right way for a parent to deal with sibling abuse? There may not be a single correct answer. Depending on the situation, any number of responses might be appropriate. One possibility is the problem-solving approach referred to here as SAFE—the safe way to deal with rivalry that is becoming perilously close to abuse. It need not be used every time siblings fight or squabble. Instead, it should be employed when parents see a *pattern* of abuse, or when a single serious episode of any type of abuse occurs. The SAFE approach involves the following steps, as each letter implies:

S: Set the scene for problem-solving
A: Assess the facts and feelings
F: Find out what works and do it
E: Evaluate whether it's working

S: Set the Scene for Problem-Solving

When parents discover trouble among their children, the first thing they need to do is create an atmosphere for problem-solving. The heat of the moment is usually not a good time, as charges and countercharges are probably still flying from one child to another. Siblings, and their parents, may need some time to cool off. It's a good idea to separate the children for an hour or so to defuse matters, then discuss the problem in a calm setting, like around the kitchen table, or in the living room.

A: Assess the Facts and Feelings

In this step, parents try to find out what happened. The children can provide some information, but parents should also look at the facts surrounding the incident, similar previous incidents, the role each sibling played, events leading up to the problem, and the impact on the victim.

In telling their side of the story, children will usually say things like, "Tommy hit me," or "Mary called me a bad name." One tactic parents can use to help sort things out is to tell the children to speak only in "I statements." This means that each sentence must start with the word *I*. Now, for example, Tommy will say, "I teased Mary and she called me a bad name." Or, Mary will say, "I hit Tommy after he hit me." This forces children to focus on what they did to contribute to the problem rather than letting them blame it all on their brothers or sisters. Making children use I statements may also result in some pretty funny sentences, which can help reduce the tension in the air.

While it's important to find out the facts surrounding an incident, it's also important to identify the *feelings* around it. Having a favorite toy ruined or being called a name may not seem important, but the feelings of the children involved may be very significant indeed.

F: Find Out What Works and Do It

After assessing the facts and feelings, parents should summarize what happened. The statement should be as brief as possible. Consider this scenario: Tim took Jennifer's bicycle and rode it to a friend's house without asking for permission to do so. Later, when he returned home with the bicycle, Jennifer was very angry. The siblings started shoving, pushing, and calling each other names. Tim and Jennifer's mother decided to use the problem-solving approach because Tim had been inconsiderate of his sister's feelings frequently in the last several weeks. After assessing what happened, their mother made the following restatement: "Tim took Jennifer's bicycle without asking her permission to do so. Jennifer was upset that her bicycle was missing when she wanted to use it."

The purpose of the problem-solving process is not for parents to sit in judgment on their children. Rather, it is to show children that their problems can be solved without violence or ridicule, and that there are better ways to work through their problems.

In this phase, parents and siblings discuss how the trouble could have been avoided. Then they set a goal to prevent the problem from occurring again. Using the example above, Jennifer, Tim, and their mother set this goal: "Each person's possessions should be respected, which means that permission must be given before using something that belongs to someone else."

At this stage, parents and siblings figure out other solutions to the problem that caused the incident. For instance, if Tim had asked Jennifer's permission to use the bicycle, the argument could have been avoided. Equally, both children should be taught to discuss their anger rather than resort to name-calling, which only makes matters worse. Further, in this step, the siblings agree—with their parents' assistance—on how they should behave. This agreement, or contract, sets out appropriate behavior to avoid and resolve problems like the one that caused the incident. Parents may also tell their children the consequences of not following the contract—such as being sent to their rooms, or denied permission to watch television, and so on. In Tim and Jennifer's case, they should establish a contract on respecting each other's property and asking for permission to use something that doesn't belong to them.

E: Evaluate Whether It's Working

Parents and children now attempt to implement the contract whenever it applies. Implementing contracts between warring siblings is not an easy task. It's much easier for children to scream and hit one another than to remember their agreements. If problems continue to arise, the contract must be reevaluated. It may need to be modified under certain conditions. If there is still no peace in the household, parents may need to help children identify what part of the agreement they keep breaking and why. Children also need to know that their abusive behavior will not be tolerated, and that it will have consequences. If problems still continue, further modifications can be made to keep the contract helpful and up-to-date.

Initially, parents may be horrified at the number of steps and time involved in this problem-solving approach. But this method is not intended for frequent use. It should be used when a serious incident occurs or a pattern of behavior can be seen. And, it does not need to take a long time—the process can be accomplished in fifteen minutes.

This approach is not a cure for all sibling problems. It does require effort on the part of both parents and siblings. Name-calling, nasty comments, and even physical abuse can sometimes be easier to accept. But there is a high emotional cost for such behavior, and unresolved problems continue to be raised again and again. The old saying that "an ounce of prevention is worth a pound of cure" is all too true, and solving problems can mean a great deal for children while they are young and in the years to come.

Understanding Sibling Abuse

For many people, the whole idea of sibling abuse is so horrifying and so strange that they are unable to make sense of it. In truth, the only way to prevent or treat sibling abuse is to understand it, and that is the focus of this chapter.

In trying to grasp the reasons behind any behavior, people often search for one simple explanation. For example, popular wisdom says that all juvenile delinquents come from broken homes, which is untrue. Perhaps a greater percentage of them do come from divorced families, but not all of them. Equally, not all children of divorce become juvenile delinquents. So, as comforting as it would be to have one explanation for our social ills, it simply doesn't work that way. Thus, just as not all juvenile delinquents come from broken homes, not all sibling abuse arises in a particular type of family.

This chapter attempts to explain sibling abuse by looking at survivors' experiences, their parents' responses, and the effects of the abuse they received. The reasons for sibling abuse given here are not the only ones; other, unexplored factors may as well have played a causal role. Also, the various "ingredients" of sibling abuse may combine in complex and different ways for each victim.

The reasons examined here are not excuses for abusive behavior. They are attempts to understand what causes abuse so those factors can be changed and the behavior ended. And, while the current trend in American society is to blame social problems on addictions and diseases, sibling abuse is not a disease or an addiction. It is destructive behavior, which can and must be changed.

Inappropriate Expectations

Abuse seems to happen most often when older siblings are left in charge of younger ones. Older children are often asked to baby-sit while their parents are working or are out for the evening. But the root cause of the abuse, in these cases, is not baby-sitting; it is the parents' inappropriate expectation that older siblings will not abuse their role. Parents also believe, sometimes unwisely, that children are mature enough, and tolerant enough, to take care of their younger brothers and sisters.

These beliefs also play a role in child abuse by adults. Abusive parents often want their children to act like adults; they have unrealistic expectations of them. They are frustrated and angry when their children act like children. The same may be true of abusive siblings. Although their parents expect them to care for younger children, they may lack the maturity, wisdom, and skills to do so. Parenting can be hard work for adults; it is even harder for children. Asking them to baby-sit may lead to trouble. The comments of respondents abused by siblings in their parents' absence are evidence of this problem.

A Massachusetts woman, forty-three years old, described the following scene, which was typical of her early childhood:

> When my parents went out dancing or to my aunt's home on a Saturday night, my two older brothers baby-sat us six children. Not long after they left, my brothers would tell us to go to bed. It was too early, so we didn't want to go to bed. When we resisted, we were hit. I was punched and slapped by my oldest brother. If I defended myself by hitting back, my oldest brother would grab my wrists in the air as he screamed at me that he would hit me more. He would be telling me what to do and to go to bed. I would be crying hard even more and would go to bed.

This victim told her parents what was happening, and they instructed her brothers to allow the children to stay up. But the physical abuse persisted and then became sexual. When she was ten years old, she told her parents that she had been molested by one of her brothers. Her parents then hired a baby-sitter whenever they went out for the evening.

Another survivor wrote:

My mother would go to bingo leaving my sister (three years older) in charge with specific chores to be done. She would make us do the work. If it didn't get done when she said, she would hit us with a belt. Leaving her in charge gave her every right to do whatever she wanted.

Another woman wrote that her brother—who was five years older than she was—was always left in charge when her parents went away for an evening.

He would constantly be telling me to do something for him—that is, ordering me around, like to change TV channels, get him a soda pop, make popcorn, get him a sandwich, etc. My refusal or sometimes just being too slow to comply would merit me being hit, usually open-handed, but sometimes with a closed fist.

An Ohio respondent described what happened after her mother died and she was left in the care of an older brother:

My father would go to work or out on a date, and my brother would be watching TV. I would be in my room, and he would come to my room with a stick and some cord. He would beat me with the stick and then tie my feet together. If I screamed too loud, he would put a scarf in my mouth or tie it around my mouth. . . . Once he took a big pot of boiling water and poured it on my hand. He did so much to me, I've blocked some of it out of my mind.

Why do some older siblings use abuse to control the younger children in their care? One reason may be that their parents use the same tactics. And, even if their parents aren't abusive, older siblings may not be mature enough to know how to deal with younger children without using force. There is nothing wrong with leaving older children in charge, *if those children can handle the responsibility*. But parents must set some standards for the child in charge and the ones being watched. They must also listen carefully when the younger children complain about this situation—they may be trying to say something very important. Negative or curt responses to these children can place them in a very vulnerable position every time their parents go out.

When Parents Are Overwhelmed by Their Own Problems

Answers to the questionnaire also suggest that sibling abuse is more likely to happen when parents are overwhelmed by their own problems. They may not have the energy or the ability to handle the situation—even if they are aware of it. Some of the parents of the survivors in this book were coping with alcoholism, mental illness, and troubled marriages, and these seemed to prevent them from stopping the abuse among their children.

A survivor from Nevada described the chaotic conditions in her childhood home:

> My mother was never home for eight or nine . . . of my most important years. She probably wasn't aware of too much in our home, as she was drinking. She'd stay away for weeks at a time and leave us there with my brother ten years older.

A similar situation was reported by a California woman:

> My family was very chaotic. My father was an alcoholic. My mother died when I was eleven years old. My father had many lovers and was gone a lot of the time.

The older sister of a Washington survivor was abusive despite her mother's efforts to prevent it. The victim's father had his own problems.

> My father was always too drunk to take note [of her abuse] or gone to the local tavern getting drunker.

Parents struggling with chronic mental or physical illness may be too tired and stressed to do anything more than leave their youngest children in the care of older siblings. This was certainly the situation faced by a Pennsylvania woman.

> I don't think my mother knew how badly I was being hurt [by an older sister], and I was afraid to tell her for fear of retaliation. She was busy trying to survive on practically nothing and deal with her own emotional problems, and probably she had systemic lupus then, even though it wasn't diagnosed for another fifteen years or so. But I think she didn't want to know how bad things were because she was powerless enough to change her circumstances.

Some people wrote that their fathers worked two jobs to support the family and so were unaware of what was happening at home. Others said that both parents worked because the paycheck from one job was never enough.

Some parents may have been physically in the home, but absent from it emotionally. A study of sexually abused siblings found that most of their parents were either out of the house or emotionally unavailable. Interviews with their parents found that many of the fathers were visibly uninterested in parenting, were not close to their children, and resented the relationship between their wives and children. These fathers did not empathize with their children, were unaware of how children develop, and felt they had little to contribute to their offspring. Many of the mothers also felt distant from their children, but not as much as the fathers in these cases.

Parents, however, have problems of their own, and sibling abuse must be seen within that framework. For example, poor job training may mean that parents have to work more than one job in order to make ends meet. Too little affordable housing may mean that brothers and sisters of different ages may have to share a room when they need privacy. Therapy may be too expensive for parents who need it. Latchkey programs for children who come home from school before their parents return from work may not be available. These and other difficult social circumstances affect entire families. It influences how children relate to their parents, and to their siblings.

Thus, solving the problem of sibling abuse and other forms of family violence—child abuse, spouse abuse, and elder abuse— involves more than just working with families. It demands that wider social ills be addressed as well. Affordable housing, day care, latchkey programs, mental health programs, and social service programs all could go a long way toward ending abuse within families.

How Victims Contribute

As previously mentioned, another factor that helps cause sibling abuse is the contribution victims make to it. This is particularly true of physical and emotional abuse.

When adults abuse children, they may not mistreat all the children in the family. Frequently, they abuse only one specific child, whose physical or behavioral characteristics make him or her a more likely target of abuse. In these cases, abuse follows a terrible and increasing cycle. Children may act in a way that prompts their parents to become abusive, which reinforces how those children behave, which in turn prompts more and worse abuse.

Research supports the idea that abused children *sometimes* seem to invite further abuse. But it is important to note that children are not to *blame* for their abuse. No one deserves to be abused—emotionally, physically, or sexually.

Some siblings may be more prone to abuse because of physical traits like weight, height, skin problems, and so on. Equally, some children may be targets of abuse because of the way they act. For example, when young children constantly demand the attention, clothes, and toys of their older brothers and sisters, it may raise tempers. Again, these children are not at fault, but their parents should be aware of what is happening and help to settle matters. Using the problem-solving approach outlined in the previous chapter may be one effective way to intervene.

Another factor that can cause sibling abuse is the emotional makeup of the abusers. Research suggests that some children have poor impulse control and are aggressive because of their own underlying rage. Unless such children receive professional help, they are a danger to themselves and to others.

Ineffective Interventions

Sometimes sibling abuse is caused—and continued—simply because parents don't know how to stop it. It's not that they don't care or are uninterested in the problem, but some parents try to change matters in ways that simply don't work. As a result, the abuse continues, and sometimes it increases. Yelling, name-calling, nasty comments, and hitting probably occur between siblings in all families—they are not abnormal and generally are stopped when parents use the right tactics. One such tactic could be the problem-solving approach discussed in the last chapter.

Ineffective interventions—like those outlined in the previous chapter—don't stop sibling abuse. Victims and abusers alike aren't taught how to avoid problem behaviors and find alternative solutions. When abusers are violently punished, things may even get worse. They get angry at their victims for reporting what happened, and increase their abuse. Victims, in turn, become too frightened to tell their parents anything.

Victims may also be afraid of what will happen to their abusers if the truth comes out. One woman told her parents that she was being physically abused by her brothers—and learned never to tell them again.

> My older brothers received a severe beating when I told my parents how they were abusing me. The severity of the beating, however, discouraged me from ever reporting again what happened because I wanted to avoid a more violent outcome.

A similar reason was voiced by a Tennessee woman who was reluctant to tell her parents about her brother's abuse.

> There would have been more beatings for everyone all around. Instead of a constant at-random sort of violence, there would have been a concerted and pointed effort to make people even more miserable.

This comment illustrates two basic principles in the "theory of violence." One, violence tends to create more violence; and violence of one type tends to spread to other types. Beating up the abusers in order to stop them from hurting their siblings just creates more tension and violence. Some people described their childhood home as a "battleground." In these cases, verbal and physical assaults are a normal pattern of behavior among family members.

> My parents were so busy abusing themselves and each other and us that it was a part of our everyday life.

> My mother abused me physically and emotionally also. She thought I deserved beatings from her and my sister.

> My parents abused me as bad if not worse than my brothers did. I would miss weeks of school at a time because of bruises, black eyes, etc. I didn't think they would be able to stop my brothers from hurting me when they did it themselves.

Physical abuse that involves whole families supports the "intergenerational theory of abuse." This theory states that parents abuse their children because they were abused themselves. Basically, the parents act the same way that their parents did—and their children may be avid learners as well.

If it is true that victims of abuse in turn abuse other people, then the existence of sibling abuse becomes even more frightening. The same siblings who abused their brothers and sisters are, according to the theory, likely to abuse their children as well. And, unless victims seek help, they may also abuse their children. Unless the cycle is broken, it can be repeated and repeated and repeated. This survivor of her brother's physical abuse shows how the cycle works:

> The worst fights started around the time I was in third grade. I got a lot of abuse from my older brother. Then I would turn around and abuse my sister. I would get her twice as hard as what I received. As we got older it got worse.

While some siblings learn cruelty from their parents, not all siblings abuse each other because their parents abuse them. Parental abuse—like all the other factors involved in sibling abuse—is not solely to blame. In fact, only a small number of people who answered the questionnaire were abused by their parents as well as their siblings.

When Abuse Seems Normal

Some parents accept abuse among their siblings because they think it is normal. They believe the aggressive sibling is "going through a phase." They excuse the behavior as normal for males, or put it down to nothing more than sibling rivalry.

A woman receiving help for problems related to sibling abuse came to the following conclusion:

> I truly thought it [the abuse] was "normal" until last year.

A Washington survivor wrote:

> The abuse was considered normal behavior by my parents, who had no idea what normal might be. I might add that the physical abuse by my siblings was much less than the emotional and sexual abuse by them.

Sibling rivalry has been around for as long as girls have had brothers and boys have had sisters. Literature is filled with examples of siblings attacking one another; the biblical story of Cain and Abel is just one. The fact that sibling rivalry is so universal often contributes to the belief that sibling abuse is normal. In fact, rivalry is normal, but abuse is not. A careful distinction must be made between the two. Telling the difference between normal and abusive behavior is the subject of chapter 8.

Why do siblings become rivals? According to Adele Faber and Elaine Mazlish in *Siblings without Rivalry (How to Help Your Children Live Together So You Can Live, Too)*, the presence of another child in the home casts a shadow on the life of the first child. Younger siblings are seen as threats to their well-being. Another child means there will be *less* for the first child—less attention from parents, less time with parents, less energy for parents to meet the first child's needs. The oldest child may even think that parents love the second child more. In short, new siblings are seen as a threat by the firstborns. Psychologist Alfred Adler calls the birth of the second child a "de-throning" of the first child.

When parents look at sibling rivalry from this perspective, they may have a better idea of how to prevent it from becoming abusive. Each child needs to be reassured that he or she is special, important, and loved. To paraphrase authors Adele Faber and Elaine Mazlish, children don't need to be treated equally, they need to be treated uniquely. Children may not need equal amounts of attention—some may need much more than others, and they should get it.

In short, parents have to work at reducing—not increasing—the natural competition between siblings. The hostile feelings between siblings can be expressed safely through the problem-solving approach; or they can be driven underground and under pressure until they finally explode. Cooperation—or fighting and abuse— between brothers and sisters can be promoted by parents. Violently punishing the abusers only makes matters worse, and sets the roles of victim and abuser in concrete. As a New York respondent wrote, sibling abuse is a learned behavior; it does not occur in a vacuum. It may be learned from other children at school, from TV where violence is often used to resolve problems, or from parents.

When Abuse Expresses Anger

Another reason siblings abuse one another is to express anger. And, if they feel like failures in one area of their lives—like school—they may see abuse as a way to regain their power and self-esteem. An Indiana respondent noted that

> My oldest brother would come in from school agitated and start literally pushing me and my brothers around. If I spoke at all I was threatened to "shut my mouth." If I cried, he would slap me or shove me down.

A Texan described a similar situation in her home with two older brothers:

> My brothers always seemed mad. It never took very much to make them hurt me. It seemed to start if I made a mistake—i.e., said something wrong, turned the TV, or needed something. Then they would yell and call me names. It usually started with them hitting me with their fists. If time allowed they used other things such as sticks, belts, razors, and knives.

Victims develop a keen sense of when their siblings are in a dangerous mood. They become sensitive to changes in temper, even when it doesn't involve them. They learn to "seek shelter," hiding from their siblings like they would from an incoming tornado. They know from experience that they could easily become the object of their siblings' growing anger. That anger is often first expressed verbally, and then physically.

This way of handling anger is sometimes seen—and accepted—as "letting off steam." The problem with this view, and this phrase, is that it looks at the venting of anger as a natural act—as if a person has no more control than a kettle of boiling water. Some therapists believe venting is a healthy way of dealing with anger. But the target of such venting should be something like a punching bag, a golf ball, or a football; not a wife, a sister, a brother, or a child.

Actually, research shows that venting anger does not make it vanish—it *increases* it. One study was of children who were encouraged to be aggressive when the mood struck and who became more and more hostile over time. Other research notes that couples who vent their anger by shouting at each other felt angrier after doing so, not calmer.

Anger is seen, in this society, as a concrete object or force that needs discharging—not as an emotional concept. In a sense, it has taken on a life of its own. In *Anger: The Misunderstood Emotion,* author Carol Tavris notes that discussing problems is a lot more effective than yelling about them. Using the problem-solving approach forces people to think through and express their feelings in a way that is constructive. Screaming at, or hitting someone else does not provide a way to avoid a similar problem in the future.

How Boys Are Brought Up

The largest percentage of people responding to the questionnaire were women who had been physically, emotionally, or sexually abused by their brothers. A common theme in their memories was the domination of brothers over sisters. And, even though our society is making an effort to change matters, children often have problems with one another because males are brought up, or socialized, to believe they have the right to control females.

Historically, women have been considered the property of men. Men believed they could treat women as they wish. The Bible, taken literally, supports a superior attitude in males. Art, literature, cartoons, and TV programs also have contributed to this problem. The different socialization of boys and girls can still be seen in the toys, games, and sports associated with each sex. Society strengthens these attitudes in adulthood, when women who do the same work as men are likely to be paid less and still end up doing all or most of the housekeeping as well.

The effects of these attitudes are clearly defined in spouse abuse. Men who beat their wives are often prompted to do so because they believe they must control and dominate them. A study of 900 randomly selected California women found that more than twice as many of them were sexually assaulted by their husbands than were assaulted by strangers. The important fact to take from this study is that abuse within the family is much more common than abuse from outside it.

Equally, the comments of the female survivors of sibling abuse in this book support the idea that their brothers believed they were supposed to be in charge. Physical and verbal abuse were seen as appropriate ways to achieve this goal. In instances of sexual abuse, brothers may have viewed their sisters as sexual objects rather than individuals, but sex can also be a form of domination. In Susan Brownmiller's book *Against Our Will* it is noted that "rape is not an aggressive expression of sexuality, but a sexual expression of aggression."

It is convenient to discuss the factors that contribute to sibling abuse separately. But in fact, they can—and do—overlap, a situation that exacerbates the lasting effects seen in this form of abuse.

7

Lasting Effects

When abused siblings grow up, leave the home, and establish their own lives, their problems are still not over. Contrary to the old saying, time does *not* heal all wounds—at least not for everyone. Physical, emotional, and sexual abuse can have terrible and permanent effects on victims—whether they were abused by parents, siblings, or strangers makes no difference. The emotional pain caused by abuse never seems to go away completely, even when survivors seek professional help for it. They may learn to cope with the pain, but the memory does not disappear. One woman explained:

> I get so angry just thinking about how humiliating and degrading this was. And my brother has been dead for twenty years.

People responding to the questionnaire had been asked how their childhood sibling abuse affects them as adults. They were asked this three times, once each for the three types of abuse—physical, emotional, and sexual. In this chapter survivors discuss how their abuse still haunts them, sometimes after thirty, forty, or more years.

Low Self-Esteem

Nearly everyone who responded to the research noted that they had low self-esteem. In fact, self-esteem appears to suffer from every type of abuse, whether from a sibling or an adult. When adults are abusive, research shows that their children tend to feel unwanted, inferior, unloved, and inadequate. Children abused by their siblings feel much the same way.

> If someone says something hurtful or gets angry, I think they will stop loving me.

I lack self-esteem and self-confidence. I cling to my husband and am afraid of a lot of things.

The emotional abuse has affected my self-esteem severely, as well as my ability to trust others.

I am insecure of my abilities. I lack assertiveness for fear I might verbally be assaulted.

One woman was constantly belittled by her older brother and sister who delighted in telling her she was unwanted. Her mother either ignored the abuse or didn't enforce her requests that it stop. This survivor now says that, as an adult

I have little confidence in my ability to be genuinely liked or to do something correctly.

Another woman, emotionally abused by two older brothers, stated:

The abuse contributed to my low self-esteem and self-confidence. I still have difficulty accepting credit for successes. I have a continuing sense of being worthless and unlovable, despite evidence to the contrary.

Absolute feelings of unworthiness are expressed by this survivor:

I feel unwanted, unloved. I feel like no one could love me. I feel no one needs or wants me. I feel like no one cares!

When victims are called nasty names, or belittled, their low self-esteem is reflected in the image they have of their bodies. Many of the names these children were called focused on things like their weight or attractiveness.

A woman whose older brother told her repeatedly that she was ugly, too tall, and fat, wrote:

I have a hard time believing I am a slender, attractive woman. At times I feel that I'm fat and ugly, but I know I'm not.

Similarly, a respondent from Ohio:

I grew up hearing how "fat" or "chubby" I was and grew up believing it. Now even when I'm thin I feel fat.

Another woman feels this way about herself:

I have low self-esteem. I feel that I'm not smart. I feel that I'm fat and ugly.

At thirty-nine, the survivor who was called "cow" by a brother because of her weight problem is still affected by it.

I think part of my weight and eating disorder problems are from believing I was a cow and cows are fat. I have a low self-image and self-worth, and at one time they were so low, I didn't believe anyone would care if I was alive or not. I'm still on antidepressants.

A woman who was sexually abused by her older brother:

I have severe bouts of extreme self-hate.

Children who were sexually abused by siblings often feel worthless, guilty, and shameful—a combination that usually results in their blaming themselves for what happened. This survivor tried to cope with her low feelings of self-worth:

I felt dirty, as I sought baptism and religious experiences to cleanse me.

Although low self-esteem is a significant consequence of sibling abuse, it is not the only lasting effect felt by survivors.

Problems with the Opposite Sex

Women who were physically, emotionally, or sexually abused by a brother often have problems in their relationships with—and attitudes toward—men. They may be distrustful, suspicious, fearful, and even hateful. Victims of their brothers, these women may now hold all men in the same regard. This has affected their ability to relate to men and has made it particularly hard to form intimate relationships with them. Some have decided not to marry. In the words of one woman:

I am uncertain of men's real intentions. I see them as a source of pain.

A North Carolina woman, physically abused by her brother and too intimidated to tell her parents, wrote that now

I have no tolerance for men and am afraid of them.

One woman who was abused by her older brother finally discussed her childhood with her mother. Her mother confirmed that the abuse had begun as soon as she came home from the maternity ward. This respondent described the effect the abuse has had on her life:

I continue to be constantly on the alert toward certain men and have difficulty controlling the instinctive fear and anger that I feel.

A similar feeling was voiced by an Idaho woman:

Other than my husband, I am not comfortable in the presence of any man in any given situation without knowing I have a way out.

A single woman, thirty-four, physically abused by her older brother and her foster brother, stated:

I do not trust men. . . . I wish I could get along in life without them.

A California respondent:

I have a lot of fear of men and tend to use my mind and intellect to push men away and intimidate them the same way I was intimidated. I have a lot of difficulties in my relationships with men. I tend to disagree a lot and to be very afraid/contemptuous of a man's need for me.

A Chicago woman:

I do not trust men. I fear them. I have been unable to marry. I choose inadequate men to be involved with. I have a fear of intimacy.

If they do marry, female victims often feel their childhood abuse has affected their marriage. One woman finds it difficult not to view her husband like her emotionally abusive brothers:

I overreact to my husband's actions. Sometimes I doubt his motives for doing things, and I accuse him of being like my brothers. I learned not to trust men. I believed they were all evil.

An underlying fear and suspicion of men is common among female survivors. They may feel cornered or trapped among men, which may come from being physically restrained while being abused or, literally, "caught" in a family unable or unwilling to stop their abuse.

Some victims have turned their abuse by men into conflicts with their faith. In most religions, God is depicted in masculine terms. Many women found it difficult to think of God as loving, kind, good—and male. Their relationships with their brothers, and even their fathers, simply did not support that idea. One woman, seriously physically abused by her older brother, is extremely afraid of men. This fear impacts on her religious views:

> Prior to more than three years of counseling intervention, . . . my concept of God was very warped. I saw Him as someone who was out to destroy or terrorize me.

For female survivors of sexual abuse, the impact on their relationships with men has been troublesome. A Louisiana woman wrote:

> I have difficulty trusting others in relationships. I am also very competitive with men and feel that I have to prove to myself that I am equal.

A respondent from Washington noted:

> I feel angry with men, like all men will hurt you sexually. I feel like I owe them sex and I can use it to keep men. Sex is my tool.

A woman from New Jersey explained:

> Deep emotional or intimate relations with men are difficult. I feel as if they are only trying to control me mentally and sex is just another form of male domination.

Another survivor is unable to relate to men because her emotional abuse "has completely destroyed any possibility of closeness or intimacy with a man."

One woman noted:

> I have developed a very strong mind, which I often use as a weapon with men to push them away. I am very vulnerable to intrusiveness and humiliation, and so I tend either to distance myself or to pick men who are distant or nonintrusive. Yet all the men I have been with have a sadistic streak similar to my brother's abuse—only it doesn't show

on the surface as much. My brother's abuse of me came out of a tremendous amount of pain, so I tend to pick men who are in a lot of pain, too.

Sibling abuse seems to have a similar effect on male survivors. A man, thirty-six years old, found his marriage suffered from it.

It ruined whatever self-esteem and self-worth I could muster. It drove me away from people in school, thinking no one would like me or love me if they knew the real me. This attitude is still prevalent today. This, combined with the parental emotional abuse, has just about ruined my life totally. It has affected my marriage immeasurably because I feel like if I get close, I'll get hurt. So right now, thirteen years into marriage, I honestly haven't got an intimate relationship.

A middle-aged man, physically abused by his older brother, feels his marriage was lost due to his childhood problems:

I was a victim. As an adult I created another victim. All the anger and resentment I had in me I took out on my wife. She took all she could take. She is now divorcing me. I've lost the best thing that ever happened to me.

Problems such as these are all too common in the adult lives of both male and female survivors of sibling abuse.

Difficulties with Relationships

Some survivors have problems in their relationships with all people, not just adult members of the opposite sex. One woman wrote that because of her childhood abuse she "often has been too hard" on her own son, and that has affected their relationship. She is also one of several people who said they would only have one child, to avoid the possibility of sibling abuse. She notes:

It is hard for me not to repeat patterns of learned behavior. The verbal abuse is the hardest one for me to stop. I'm very aware of defending my boundaries. I'm still struggling to give my son his own boundaries; however, my son and I have continued therapy to help us individuate. I'm too fearful of enmeshment and repeating earlier cycles to rely on my subjectivity . . . to intercept what I'm too close to see. I doubt my parenting ability.

The difficulty that survivors have in their relationships often relates to their low self-esteem. However, the more poor relationships people have, the lower their self-esteem gets, and this creates an ever worsening cycle. The comments that follow illustrate some of the problems. One respondent:

I do not stand up for myself. I accept things without questioning.

A survivor of physical abuse states:

I still have a tendency to avoid conflict, back off, and clam up.

Suspicion and distrust are also leftovers of an abused childhood. One person wrote:

I'm afraid that everyone is going to abuse me in some way. I don't trust anyone. I feel in everything people say and do that they want to hurt me. I always want to take the blame for any mistake made, or I feel that everyone is blaming me.

A Washington woman described how being abused has affected her adult relationships:

I find it difficult to relate to others. I am not afraid of people or hate them. I merely find no desire to reach out to others socially or emotionally. Mostly, I simply want to be left alone—except, of course, for my husband and two sons. We are extremely close and happy.

A middle-aged divorced woman, abused by an older and a younger sister, realizes

I'm angry. I feel my self-esteem has been diminished. I act out in more sophisticated, socially acceptable ways. My anger is directed toward peers at work as though they were my sisters.

Also abused by an older sister, this Washington resident believes

It has made me very cynical—untrusting of those who attempt to get close quickly. I grew up feeling if your own family doesn't like or want you, who will?

Survivors of emotional abuse who verbally fought back often feel that it has affected the way they communicate with other adults. One such person wrote:

I still have an abusive tongue. My mouth is a big weapon. It keeps people at a distance.

Equally, the survivors of physical abuse often feel a lasting impact on their ability to touch or be touched by other adults, even in a friendly, nonsexual way. Two adult women wrote:

I get very afraid and shrivel when anyone is physically forceful with me. Even if they are being playful or roughhousing, I get terribly upset and tremble.

When I'm frustrated, I tend to gently or playfully slug the person. I have a hard time touching people without it being a playful bop or light punch in the arm. When I do hug someone, I'm very wimpy because I'm afraid my touch will hurt them.

A woman who was physically abused by an older brother and younger sister had difficulty with her relationships in college. Now twenty-seven, she believes the problems stemmed from sibling abuse in childhood:

It took me until my third year of college to really realize and get under control my own rage when frustrated—to really act upon not yelling at my roommates, threatening them, or throwing adult temper tantrums.

Difficulties in dealing with people can make it hard to hold a job or build a career.

I believed my needs were not important. I believed I had nothing to offer anyone. It is impossible for me to trust. Holding on to a job has been very difficult. I expect friends, boyfriends, and employers to treat me as my brother did. I struggle in almost all aspects of life.

Another problem that survivors may have is an endless desire to be approved of and to please other people. They may end up trying too hard, and that can interfere with their relationships as well.

A Midwestern woman, who holds a graduate degree, was the target of emotional abuse from an older and younger brother. She explains:

Until I went into psychotherapy one year ago, I did everything I could to be approved of by my family—worked all the time, spent money for their needs at special occasions, etc., just to have them tell me I was okay. They continued to downgrade my profession and my education. I was always trying to be perfect and took all responsibility for my family. Unfortunately, I married someone who had two adult children who treated me as my brothers did, and I went through the same dance for them, too.

At times, feelings of anger explode at inappropriate targets. A respondent from Maine wrote:

I have a tremendous amount of suppressed anger that erupts occasionally.

A New York woman has struggled for years to control her rage but at times has lashed out unfairly at friends and associates. She also says,

I am afraid to think about having children. I'm afraid I may lose control one day and really hurt my own kids.

These accounts of survivors tell of only some of the many different ways childhood abuse affects adult relationships.

Repeating the Victim Role

A significant effect of sibling abuse—especially physical, but also emotional and sexual—is that victims tend to repeat the victim role in adult relationships. They choose friends and spouses who abuse them. This, in turn, reinforces their low self-esteem and feelings of worthlessness. In a terrible sense, they make themselves "right" about not deserving more than an abusive relationship.

A woman who was abused by an older brother reflected on her childhood and the impact it has had on her adult life.

I now know that my brother hurt me because he needed something desperately from me that he felt he didn't have himself. He felt weaker than me. I tend to pick men now who are weaker than me and need a lot. Then I push them away. I also pick men who have a covert sadistic streak.

A girl abused by her brother or sister may grow up to marry a man who abuses her. In the case of a California woman:

It took me into my thirties before I began to see a pattern from it [the abuse].... I chose a first husband who abused me. Also, I tend to constantly be doing too much, as if to make me feel better.

Two other women wrote:

The abuse from my childhood made me think that was normal. It made me stay in an abusive adult relationship and think it wasn't so bad. It took a long, long time until I was able to call for the police to come to our home, and then only after much counseling.

Being abused by someone I thought I was supposed to love set me up for further abuse from mates. I developed very unhealthy boundaries. I suffered through three years of abuse in my first marriage.

These comments indicate that people who were abused as children often believe that abuse is normal. Unless they have other people to use as role models—like friendly siblings and happy families—they may think that everyone is abused or abusive. One respondent voiced these feelings:

The abuse I experienced as a child from a sibling made me think that was normal, that I deserved it. I still find myself getting into abusive relationships. The abuse I experienced made me not trust people. I have low self-esteem and feel shame.

Research on survivors of incest shows that they are likely to continue being abused as adults. Child sexual abuse victims may come to believe that abusive relationships are standard, so they choose mates who abuse them as well. Similarly, battered wives often leave one abusive relationship only to enter another, becoming endless victims.

Therapy and support groups are excellent places for victims to realize that abuse is abnormal.

Overly Sensitive

Sibling abuse victims often describe themselves as "overly sensitive." This is particularly true of survivors of emotional abuse and is probably related to the ridicule and degradation of their childhoods. As adults, they seem to expect their abuse to continue, so they may look for hidden negative meanings behind the positive messages they receive in life.

> No matter what compliments I receive or deeds I accomplish, I continue to feel like a hopeless, incompetent person. I am very sensitive to criticism. I do not trust others nor expect them to like me. So I have few friends and seldom share my feelings with others. I am frequently depressed and have planned numerous suicide routes, though I never attempted any.

> I am overly concerned with what others think of me. I need constant reaffirmation and tend to read into everything something negative or critical of myself. I get really hurt when anyone says anything remotely insensitive or critical.

> I would feel every mistake I made indicated what an awful person I was.

This last respondent stated that she has been able to cope with her hypersensitivity and low self-esteem only through therapy.

Continued Self-Blame

Victims of sibling sexual abuse often blame themselves at the time they are abused. They may continue this pattern of self-blame as adults. They find themselves repeatedly thinking that they "allowed" the abuse to occur, even though there was probably nothing they could have done about it at the time.

An Idaho woman, sexually abused by her older brother, felt responsible for the abuse and notes the impact it has left on her life.

> I was told by several women and especially by my older sister that it was my fault, because of the way I dressed and carried myself. I am very self-conscious now as an adult of how I dress. I do not like or wear short skirts. I prefer turtleneck sweaters and high-necked blouses. I do not accept compliments very well from men, other than my husband.

At the age of four, one girl was paid a quarter to perform oral sex on her brother. She did so, believing he would hurt her if she refused.

I have punished myself for twenty-two years for taking that quarter from him. I don't like myself.

An Arizona respondent also feels guilty for not having prevented her traumatic childhood. This is an example of what some mental health professionals call "stinkin' thinkin'," or an absence of reality in how victims look at what happened. In these cases, victims compare what "should" have happened with what did happen and take the blame for it. In fact, most victims were powerless to do anything about their young lives. The woman quoted above, for example, had not been taught to say no to sexual assault, and her parents did not protect her.

When parents blame victims for sexual abuse, it can be devastating. This is true at the time of the abuse, and well into adulthood. Even though survivors may know intellectually that they were helpless, emotionally they still feel guilty.

Anger

The inability to cope with anger is a problem that many survivors have in common. In describing their feelings, they often used the words *rage* and *anger*. They said they are afraid of expressing their anger, afraid of other people's anger, and afraid of their own "uncontrollable outbursts of anger." The survivors relate their present feelings with their emotions during other phases of their lives. First, they remember their fury as children whose parents didn't stop their abuse. Second, they were angry throughout their adult years, often without knowing why. And, third, they are still angry at their siblings for the abuse they suffered. Although many people have received professional help, they still feel angry.

Too many childhood victims of sibling abuse grow up to be angry adults. Some are angry in general and lash out in response to various situations. Some are angry at men—like their bosses, friends, and mates—who remind them of their siblings. For this latter group, men have come to represent the enemy—people who will hurt them if given a chance.

Respondents to the questionnaire were asked to rate their anger. Over half of them said they were "very angry," with some claiming their anger was too high to calculate.

When survivors describe how their abuse has affected their adult years, this sort of anger can be easily understood. Many have been unable to lead normal, emotionally healthy lives. Some have suffered other types of abuse, and believe that their earlier treatment made them perpetual victims. Others have spent untold hours and money on therapy—some of which was very painful—to try to cope with the effects of their abuse.

Some of the survivors, however, said they were "not at all angry" at their siblings. These people may have successfully worked through their anger, either during therapy or by other means. They have not forgotten what happened to them, but they have emotionally made peace with it. It should be noted that making peace with oneself is not the goal of therapy for all victims. Different people handle their anger in various ways, even after therapy.

Another reason why some survivors feel no anger is that they may be denying it. Research shows that children of alcoholics deny their emotions of fear, embarrassment, loneliness, and anger. In order to survive the problems and the stress created by their parents' alcoholism, they pretend to be happy and deny their emotional pain. Other people "deny" their problems simply by forgetting them. They block out certain childhood memories, things they don't want to think about. Pretending and forgetting have the same effect, a denial of reality. This denial can prevent people from seeking the professional help they need.

Survivors of incest also deny feelings of shame, guilt, despair, and anger. Perhaps if feelings are too painful to be recognized, they are denied. When children are abused by a sibling—especially sexually—they, too, may have been forced to deny their anger at what was happening to them. For example, one woman, thirty-eight years old, wrote:

> I'm realizing how sketchy my memories of my abuse are. I guess like most people, I've blocked out an awful lot of it.

Some experts believe that anger is an unavoidable response when people are taken advantage of, manipulated, or used. The ways that they deal with their anger, however, are often ineffective. They may submit silently, fight back in ways that don't work, or emotionally distance and blame themselves and others. These responses are clear in many of the comments of survivors in this book.

The survivors' anger at their siblings, and in some cases at their parents, makes it difficult for them to maintain any contact with their families. Many victims see their families very rarely because their abuse and emotional pain continues. Others stay away because seeing their families brings back terrible memories. Some have panic and anxiety attacks when they see their abusive siblings.

A survivor of sexual abuse by four older brothers wrote:

> There is still a lot of resentment toward my parents for being so irresponsible. I blame them for some of the confused feelings I have regarding sex. In fact, I blame them much more than I do my brothers because my brothers were just victims like myself.

Sexual Problems

Many survivors of sibling sexual abuse have problems in their adult sex life. They tend either to avoid all sexual contact or to become sexually promiscuous. Some female victims wrote that they really dislike sex, even, in some cases, with their husbands. One woman, whose sexual abuse began at age eight and continued several times a week during her teenage years, noted:

> I've spent eight years in therapy for sexual abuse. I still freeze up when I'm touched in the vaginal area, which makes sex very unfulfilling and has been a big factor in the breakup of my relationships.

Another respondent:

> I have been deeply affected by the sexual abuse from my brother. Even after years of therapy, it's hard for me to be truly open sexually with a man. I often experience shame and disgust around sex and tend to focus on the man's experience and pleasure rather than my own. I have a hard time initiating sex. I often experience myself as a sexual object to be used and contemptuously discarded by men.

Some survivors see their childhood sexual abuse as the reason why they are fearful and unable to marry. Two women explained:

> I am scared every man is going to make sexual advances toward me. I'm afraid of ever getting married because I'm afraid my husband might abuse me.

I feel uncomfortable with men, I do not trust them, and wonder if I will ever be able to be married to a man of excellent character and moral quality and have a healthy home life.

A woman, thirty-five years old, was raped by her brother several times a week as a child. She is certain that her adult sexuality was affected by this experience. She told her parents about the abuse, but her brother denied it. After this episode, he abused her more than ever.

The abuse made me so hate my body at so early an age that I became a transsexual and have lived as a man nearly all my adult life. I have yet to have surgery, but I still hope to. The constant rejection of my body and self by my mother—and what is abuse but rejection at its worse—is, I have no doubt, the basis of my transsexualism. And it wouldn't surprise me if it's behind far more instances of transsexualism.

Other people respond in a completely different manner, described by this female survivor from Tennessee.

I allowed others to take sexual advantage of me. I was sexually abused in my first marriage. I struggled for years with not knowing what normal, healthy, sexual experiences were.

A respondent from Texas believes her behavior was an attempt to punish men for the abuse she received from her brother.

I became very sexually active after leaving home at twenty. I did not want to have meaningful or strong relationships with anyone, but to have sex with many men and never see them again, so that they might have a feeling of being used and hurt.

Another woman had a similar experience after she left home.

I was promiscuous as a college student. I had extreme difficulty telling a man what I needed in a relationship. I felt I had to give a good performance. I had absolutely no self-confidence. I equated sex with love.

An Indiana woman described the impact of being sexually abused by a sibling:

It resulted in profound confusion about intimacy, sexuality, and my own body. It prevented me from recognizing inappropriate behavior and left me open to later abuse by others. It prevented establishment of a firm sense of boundaries, so that I have difficulty respecting and protecting my boundaries. The result is, I have spent my life either avoiding contact or in dysfunctional relationships. It resulted in numbing of emotions to avoid the painful feelings associated with the abuse.

When victims become very sexually active, they may finally feel in control of when they have sex, instead of being forced into it. However, since their siblings may have bribed them to have sex, they may still use sex to get things—attention, privileges, and so on.

A gay male survivor who was sexually abused by his older brother wrote that his childhood affected how he functioned as a homosexual.

The abuse affected me in tremendous ways. I became a doormat. My early homosexual experiences were very passive on my part. I tried to make friends by doing things for them. I spent all my money and ended up with no friends. I have difficulty with the relationship I now have. I don't relate well sexually with him. I now know I need help to deal with the child inside me.

The reactions of sexually abused siblings are not uncommon, or different from those of other survivors of the same abuse. Research shows that people who were sexually abused as children are much more likely to have sexual problems than the rest of the population. Other studies indicate that a very high percentage of male and female prostitutes were abused in this way as children.

Eating Disorders, Alcoholism, and Drug Abuse

Some survivors of sibling abuse turned to food, alcohol, and drugs. A survivor of sexual abuse from both her brother and her father associates her eating disorders with her abuse:

I have an eating disorder—bulimic—and am at times anorexic. These have to do with the denial of needs and the shame and hate I have regarding taking things into my body.

In addition to eating disorders, 25 percent of people responding to the research said they had a problem with drugs or alcohol. One respondent wrote:

I still tend to blunt my feelings or drown them in booze. I am in Alcoholics Anonymous.

Other studies show that many female drug abusers have a long history of sexual abuse; and that as many as 30 to 44 percent of people with drug and alcohol problems have been sexually abused as children.

Depression

Many survivors of sibling abuse believe that their childhood experiences contributed to their bouts of depression as adults. When asked how being sexually abused by a sibling affected her as a adult, one woman responded:

Terribly! I have seriously considered suicide. I experience severe depression requiring medication.

Studies of sexually abused children show that, as adults, they often struggle with depression. Their depression may stem from the terrible feelings of powerlessness, hopelessness, and despair that they had as children, and continue to have as adults. They feel there is nothing they can do about what happened to them, just like the victims of sibling abuse who told their parents but were ignored or not believed. One such survivor felt that same impotence when she was being sexually abused, and when her parents didn't believe her.

If you can't trust and depend on your own family members, your siblings and parents, whom can you trust?

Depression, in fact, plays such a large role in survivors' lives that 26 percent, or thirty-nine people responding to the questionnaire, had been hospitalized for depression. It seems likely that even more have sought help for depression on an out-patient basis.

Some survivors experienced such severe depression that 33 percent, or fifty people responding to the research, attempted suicide.

Other studies of survivors of sexual abuse report even higher rates of attempted suicides. While no figures are known for how many people attempt suicide nationwide, the American Association of Suicidology believes that it is probably less than one percent.

Depression and anger are closely linked. They are often called two sides of the same coin. Perhaps the only difference between them is that anger is pointed at someone else, and depression is pointed inward. This means that depression is the result of anger being internalized by victims. This seems especially true of victims who blamed themselves for the abuse they received and the fact that their parents didn't believe or protect them. It appears that the only conclusion they could reach was that they deserved to be abused. It's enough to make anyone depressed.

Flashbacks

Some people still have vivid flashbacks of their abuse by a sibling. This is especially true of victims of sexual abuse. These flashbacks often occur when they are having sex themselves.

> Until recently sexual intercourse was not very enjoyable. Well, I would enjoy it, but I could never achieve an orgasm. Sometimes sex would become so emotionally upsetting that in the middle of it, I would remember the past, and the moment would be destroyed and I'd usually cry.

Another woman:

> Sometimes I will be thinking about what my brother did to me, and when my husband approaches me for sex, I will push him away. I find myself daydreaming about the whole nightmare of my sexual abuse. It's as if it's still happening and is never going to stop.

A Missouri respondent:

> I have a great deal of difficulty in my sexual relationship with my husband. Often I have had flashbacks during sex that are debilitating.

These flashbacks are identical to the ones suffered by Vietnam veterans and other people who have lived through traumatic events. Flashbacks are a symptom of "post-traumatic stress disorder." This disorder may affect people whose lives have held more than the normal business losses, illnesses, marriage problems, and natural deaths.

Various events may evoke this stress disorder, including serious threats to people's lives or integrity, threats or harm done to family members or friends, sudden destruction of personal property, and witnessing someone being seriously injured or killed. Recently, mental health professionals have added sexual abuse by an adult to this list of horrors. It would appear that sexual abuse by a sibling should be added as well.

Survivors of sexual abuse often push what happened out of their memories and apparently forget it. This is a kind of emotional anesthesia. They may use alcohol and drugs to help the process. But, in post-traumatic stress disorder, people remember what happened in various ways. They may have flashbacks, or relive the event over and over through dreams. When something happens that resembles the problem—like having sex, or being alone in a dark room at night—they may become very distressed. Children who were sexually abused by a relative often become terribly anxious at family gatherings many years and decades later. Sometimes even an after-shave lotion that smells like the one the abuser wore can trigger an awful sense of panic.

To avoid these feelings, survivors who have post-traumatic stress disorder often limit their contact with other people. They withdraw into themselves. This is also true of many survivors of sibling sexual abuse who fear men, abstain from sex, and avoid spending time with their parents and siblings.

Positive Effects of Abuse

Some people said they were able to make the best of the sibling abuse they suffered in childhood. They are not saying that their abuse was helpful; they know they are victims of what happened, and they suffer the emotional consequences of abuse. However, they also used their abuse as a way to grow and learn.

A woman from Texas found that her experiences as a victim made her more sensitive to what children say; and she makes it clear that parents and other people who care for children can prevent sibling abuse by listening carefully to them:

In a way, my brother helped me. I've learned to listen to both sides of the story. In my job of baby-sitting for children, I've learned to realize that tattle-taling is not always true. I have learned not to discipline until I know the truth.

Another survivor has used her experiences in her work with families:

I teach family members how to be positive and to reinforce appropriate behavior as well as good family communication skills. I want to prevent emotional abuse, as I know how it feels to be a recipient!

One respondent found that the strategies she used to cope with her brother's emotional abuse have helped her personality:

I did develop a wry sense of humor, a quick wit, and a good vocabulary from the survival techniques I had to use.

Although the survivors in this book identified how their abuse affected their adult lives, many people don't realize that their childhood problems may cause chronic symptoms in adulthood. Even when they seek treatment for persistent depression and other emotional problems, they may not tell their therapists that they were abused because they don't see how it relates to anything. Survivors also may be too embarrassed or ashamed to discuss their abuse, and some therapists don't ask whether anything happened. In some cases, when the history of abuse remains hidden and untreated, therapy may not be successful.

The Difference between Normal and Abusive Behavior

Many people may empathize, or even identify with the physical pain and emotional suffering of the survivors in this book. But others may react differently. In fact, they may doubt the whole issue of sibling abuse. It's not that they think these survivors are lying, but they have difficulty deciding exactly what is abuse. They know that rape and assault and ridicule are abusive, whether it's between strangers, friends, or family members. But they are unsure whether other, less obvious types of behavior are abusive or normal for children.

All siblings hit, slap, and punch each other. All siblings call each other names. To a lesser extent, some siblings even experiment with touching and other types of sexual activity. The critical question, then, is how normal behavior is different from abusive behavior. What distinguishes harmful from harmless behavior?

Two brothers, ages eight and ten, are playing. The younger brother puts a pair of toy handcuffs on his older brother's wrists behind his back, so he can't get out of them. While his brother struggles and yells, the younger boy goes into the house for a snack. Is this physical abuse? A sister calls her brother a name— "butt-head," for example. Is this emotional abuse? A brother and sister, ages two and three, are taking a bath together. The boy notices the differences between his and his sister's genitals. He reaches over to check if she doesn't have a penis hidden somewhere. Is this sexual abuse?

The purpose of this chapter is to identify ways in which parents and other people can tell the difference between normal, abusive, and potentially abusive behaviors. However, it is important to remember that human behavior cannot always be divided cleanly among such categories. There is no comforting division between black and white in sibling actions. Human behavior is complex, and there will always be gray areas or incidents that may or may not be abusive depending on how one looks at them. Still, in cases of uncertainty, it's probably wise to protect the victim.

There are two steps that must be taken before figuring out whether or not a certain behavior is abusive. The first is to ignore the "everybody-does-it" defense. The second is to carefully examine the behavior in question.

"Everybody Does It!"

Every parent has heard the protest "Everybody does it!" when scolding or confronting their children about a particular behavior. Parents may even hold onto this phrase for comfort when telling themselves that all children fight, and hit, and call each other names. They may remember acting the same way with their siblings. In fact, they may decide that since all children seem to behave this way, it must be normal and even harmless.

It is true that all children act in these ways at some time, and to some extent. But just because many children act a certain way does not make it right, or less hurtful to their siblings. This is particularly true if their siblings are being forced to participate.

An analogy may help explain this problem. Only a few years ago, many adults in the United States smoked cigarettes. The fact that "everybody did it" didn't make tobacco less harmful. In fact, a number of behaviors that used to be acceptable are now seen as dangerous, including smoking, fraternity hazing, drinking while driving, and drug use. The phrase "everybody does it" certainly doesn't excuse or justify negative behavior.

Identify the Behavior

Before trying to distinguish whether a behavior is normal or abusive, it must be clearly identified. One way to do this is to isolate the emotions surrounding the event—like anger, hurt, or shame—from the event itself. Then the behavior can be labeled more easily. Each of the following examples illustrates a specific behavior:

> Two siblings, two and four years old, are constantly fighting over toys. Whenever the four-year-old chooses a toy to play with, the two-year-old chooses the same toy. A struggle ensues, and one of them, generally the two-year-old, ends up crying.

> Sue is fourteen years old. She is very angry because her parents only allow her to date in groups and insist that she be home by ten o'clock. But Mary, Sue's seventeen-year-old sister, is allowed to go on dates alone with a boy, and may stay out until eleven o'clock. Sue is very jealous of Mary's privileges, and every weekend she tells her parents they aren't being fair. To make matters worse, the sisters fight constantly over this issue. Recently, their parents heard Sue call Mary an "ugly bitch" after an argument about dating privileges.

> A mother notices that her four-year-old son is fascinated by his new baby sister during diaper changes. He seems very curious about her genital area and always comes running in when the baby's diapers are changed.

The behaviors in these examples were, in order, fighting, name-calling, and observation. To determine whether or not they were abusive, the first step is to look at the ages of the children involved.

Step 1. Act Your Age

The first step, or criterion, in distinguishing abusive from normal behavior is to determine whether or not the behavior is age-appropriate, or normal behavior for a child of that age. Consider the first example: It is appropriate, or normal, for two-year-olds and four-year-olds to fight over toys. The younger child is probably mimicking the older one. It is easier, and probably more fun, to do what his big brother is doing, even though his big brother doesn't think so.

In the second example, jealousy and fighting over differences in privileges is age-appropriate for teenagers. They are both figuring out who they are and trying their wings outside of the safe nest of home. Sue, at fourteen, doesn't think she is any less mature than Mary and believes they should be treated equally despite their age difference. However, name-calling is not an appropriate way to handle anger, even if it is a common one.

The observation and sexual curiosity of the four-year-old in the third example is also normal. The child who has never seen a vagina will probably ask why his sister is different "down there." If that child wants to touch his baby sister's vagina, it may be appropriate to use that as a time to explain good and bad touches. This example highlights the importance of children having sexual information that matches their age.

What is age-appropriate behavior, and how can it be determined? Child development professionals can help explain which behaviors are appropriate to the age and maturity of various children, and books on child development can help as well. Other parents are a wonderful resource, as they can share information and experiences. The parents of a mentally retarded child, for example, told their friends that their five-year-old would sometimes crawl on the floor and bark like a dog or meow like a cat. The parents saw this as an example of his retardation. The friends, however, pointed out that their five-year-old child, who was not mentally retarded, frequently did the same thing. In fact, he had once asked to be fed out of a bowl on the floor like the family pets. Thus, the first set of parents learned that this was age-appropriate behavior for a five-year-old.

On the other hand, some sibling behavior is not age-appropriate and should be considered abusive. For example, a ten-year-old boy destroys his three-year-old sister's dolls by pulling out their hair, tearing off their legs or arms, or stabbing them with a knife. An eight-year-old girl composes a song about her younger brother who is overweight. The verses make fun of him and call him "tubby." She sings it whenever she is around him, or his friends. A fourteen-year-old boy fondles the genitals of his three-year-old sister behind a shed in the backyard.

These examples show three different kinds of behavior—destruction of toys, ridicule, and sexual fondling. In light of their ages, the aggressive siblings should know better. A ten-year-old boy should have learned already to respect the toys of other children and not to destroy them. Likewise, while an eight-year-old girl may find teasing delightful, her brand of teasing is vicious because it is done in front of her brother's friends. And, a boy fondling his sister's genitals is not appropriate at any age. By fourteen, a boy should know the sexual difference between boys and girls, and between good and secret touches. The fact that he hid while fondling her is a clue that he knows he's doing something wrong. Finally, his sister is not old enough to decide if she wants to participate.

Lastly, even though fighting, jealousy, and teasing between siblings can be expected, it should not be ignored. Normal behavior can become abusive if parents don't step in and keep control of the situation. Moreover, constant fighting between siblings is unpleasant for the entire family. The question is how and when to intervene. There are a number of places where parents whose children fight all the time can get help. Parent education courses are available at many community mental health agencies, churches, community colleges, support groups, and so on. Books that focus on sibling relationships may also be helpful and can be found in bookstores and libraries. Two very helpful books are *Siblings without Rivalry* and *How to Talk So Kids Will Listen and Listen So Kids Will Talk,* both by Adele Faber and Elaine Mazlish.

Step 2. How Often and How Long Has This Been Going On?

Fighting, name-calling, teasing, and even some sexual exploration occur between most brothers and sisters at one time or another, and may be considered normal sibling rivalry and simple sexual curiosity. But the frequency and duration of a behavior may make it harmful. When fighting, name-calling, and other acts happen over and over again, they become abusive, particularly if the aggressive sibling is told to stop but continues anyway.

This doesn't mean that an abusive, or potentially abusive, event should be ignored if it happens only once. In some cases, siblings are sexually abused only once, and it affects them for the rest of their lives. The respondent who accepted money to perform oral sex on her brother, and who agreed to do so because she was scared of him, wrote:

I have punished myself for twenty-two years for taking that quarter from him. I don't like myself.

Thus, frequency and duration are not the only criteria to use in determining whether a behavior is abusive.

How long is too long, and how often is too frequently? Common sense is probably the best way to answer these questions. When a parent feels uncomfortable about a behavior, it is time to do something about it. For example, when parents want to leave the room because their children are fighting, it has gone on too long. This is especially true if it is a pattern of behavior that occurs over a period of time. Ignoring problems will not always make them disappear.

Step 3. Is There a Victim?

A victim is someone who is hurt or injured by the action or actions of another person. They are unwilling partners, or objects, in the abusive behavior. The people quoted in this book think of themselves as victims of their siblings' actions. And they are right—they were the targets of their brothers' fists, the butt of their sisters' jokes, or the object of their siblings' sexual abuse. They have not forgotten being victims. They vividly recall what happened to them ten, twenty, and even thirty years before.

Sometimes victims are people who have been duped or fooled by another person. Many of the people in this book, especially the ones who were sexually abused, became victims because they were powerless in the situation. They were enticed, threatened, or taken advantage of because of their age. They had little choice but to give in to sex because they thought there was nothing else they could do. Many of them weren't even mature enough to realize what was happening.

Victims or unwilling participants may not even be able to agree or disagree to do something. Just because they take part in something doesn't mean they did it voluntarily. Children may be unable to say no to their older sibling's sexual advances because they are too young. For example, a two-year-old child is not able to protest her older brother's sexual explorations. Likewise, a mentally retarded or emotionally disturbed adolescent who is the continual object of jokes and ridicule by a younger sibling may not be able to fend off these verbal assaults.

There is a rule of thumb for determining if children are victims of actions by their siblings. It depends on how their siblings approached them. If there was game-playing, trickery, deceit, bribery, or force involved, then the person who was the target of the behavior is a victim. For example, a four-year-old girl is bribed with candy to go to a tree-house that her brother and his friends have built behind the garage. When she gets there, she is asked to remove her panties and expose herself. Or, an older brother constantly takes money from his little brother by pretending that bigger coins are worth more. In both instances, the sibling is a victim, and the behavior is abusive.

Other clues to figuring out whether children are victims are the emotions they feel. Children called names by their siblings may be hurt or embarrassed. Sometimes the names are not upsetting to them, and that's a good sign. The important thing is to look at their emotional reactions to the name-calling, including subtle reactions.

People who have been targets of abusive behavior may not realize that they were victims until long after the fact. Young children who were sexually abused by older siblings may not realize the consequences of what occurred until much later. They may feel victimized only when they have sexual problems in their relationships, or emotional problems in general.

Victims commonly blame themselves for what happened to them. Many of the people in this book not only blamed themselves but were also blamed by their abusive siblings and parents. If these children are not protected, or are blamed, they may have trouble realizing they were victims in the first place.

Step 4. Is There a Purpose to the Behavior?

Another way to distinguish abusive from normal behavior is to look at why one sibling is acting a certain way toward another. What is the purpose of the behavior?

In most cases of emotional abuse, the purpose is to belittle victims with ridicule and name-calling. This is behavior designed to be mean or destructive, and that makes it abusive. If victims provoke their siblings, then they are both involved in the abuse and placing themselves in the roles of victim and perpetrator. They may not have learned, or remembered, appropriate ways to settle their differences. Using the problem-solving approach discussed in chapter 5 is one way to stop abusive behavior between siblings.

When older siblings—usually males—sexually abuse their younger brothers or sisters, then the purpose is their own sexual gratification and their victims' degradation. This is not the same as the four-year-old boy's curiosity and observation of his sister's genitals. It's important to note that the victims gave their abusers sexual pleasure—either through masturbation, touching, viewing, or oral sex. As the children were victims of this behavior, it is abusive.

When sex is used for sadism or suffering it is also, obviously, abusive. When older siblings insert objects into the vagina or anus of their victims, it is done to be cruel. If the older siblings also masturbate, then meanness becomes mixed with pleasure.

In some incidents of sexual abuse, there are more people involved than just the perpetrator and the victim. Younger siblings may be forced or bribed into sexual acts with their friends because it gives their older siblings pleasure. Or, one sibling may encourage another to physically or emotionally abuse a third sibling. These behaviors are also abusive because they create victims, and because they are designed for the pleasure of the perpetrators.

Children often don't realize why they do things. "I don't know" is a common reply to questions by parents. While part of that response is defensive—it may seem like the safest thing to say under the circumstances—another part of it is true. They may not be mature enough to understand what made them act a certain way. They behave on impulse, without thinking about the consequences. Also, children often don't have the experience to be able to predict bad results. They see only the action and not the effect.

Other Questions

Parents and other adults may also want to ask themselves the following questions to help identify behaviors as normal or abusive.

What were the circumstances surrounding the behavior?
What preceded the behavior?
How did the victim contribute to what happened?
Was the abuser imitating something he or she had seen?
Was the behavior planned or impulsive?
Has the behavior occurred before?
How did the victim feel about what happened?
How did the abuser feel about what happened?
Has the abuser been confronted about this behavior before?
Why did the abuser act this way?

Deciding whether a behavior was abusive or normal is not always easy. Examining the answers to these questions and going through the steps above can help. Sometimes there is no clear-cut answer, but if parents are uncomfortable with what has happened, chances are the victims are, too. The safest approach may be to decide the behavior is abusive and to make sure that changes are made in how siblings deal with one another.

Preventing Sibling Abuse

How can sibling abuse be prevented? What specifically can be done? Perhaps the experts in this field are the survivors themselves. People responding to the research were each asked to make one suggestion. Together, they came up with eight of them.

Be Aware

Nearly every respondent commented that people must be made aware of sibling abuse—that it can occur in any family, and that it is a serious problem. Many people try to distance themselves from unpleasant issues like sibling abuse and believe that it only happens in other families. They doubt it occurs in the homes of people they know and work with; they tell themselves it only happens in families on welfare living in poor housing, and in families where the parents are drunks and the kids are on drugs.

Sibling abuse may be more likely to occur in families with a lot of problems, but only families with one child can be positive it doesn't exist in their homes. The parents of the survivors in this book were quite well educated. Almost half of them attended college or graduate school. Some of them were very religious, and some were not religious at all. Thus, it's safe to assume that neither education nor religion is a guarantee against sibling abuse. A respondent from Texas wrote about the importance of religion in her family; she nevertheless experienced great emotional pain from abuse by a sibling.

> My problem and others' is that we come from religious, "looking-good" families but where there was a lot of pain and dysfunctioning on the inside.

Awareness that sibling abuse can occur in any family is the first step toward preventing it. Parents, teachers, friends, and mental health professionals must be sensitive to this type of abuse; and to its symptoms of constant fighting, or shy and withdrawn behavior by children who cling to their parents. Mental health professionals should ask about sibling abuse when they counsel adults for emotional problems. The survivors themselves may not link their behavioral, emotional, or sexual difficulties with what happened to them as children, so the facts may need to be drawn out.

A New Mexico respondent put it this way:

> We must first acknowledge that the problem of sibling abuse can occur—not minimize it or deny it. Once the potential for the problem is acknowledged, then appropriate steps can be taken to prevent the problem.

To build awareness, individuals and families must be educated about sibling abuse. Fortunately, survivors of sibling abuse are finally coming forward. Local, state, and national organizations designed to prevent child abuse can—and should—now add sibling abuse to their roster of problems. The methods used by these organizations—such as the media and abuse-prevention programs in schools—need to be modified to include sibling abuse. But the educational process must be done at many different levels and by a variety of groups, such as families, churches, schools, the military, and businesses. A survivor who grew up in a military family laments the fact that no services were provided to assist them:

> We were a military family. The military was in total denial of alcohol or other domestic problems of their enlisted people. They provided no mental health or social support systems to their families.

Teachers, as well as clergy, physicians, nurses, social workers, psychologists, psychiatrists, writers, and moviemakers, to name a few, can also help explain the issues of sibling abuse. Businesses can include short articles on it in their newsletters. Children can be introduced to it through social studies and health classes at school. Clergy can refer to it as a social dilemma, on a par with spouse abuse, elder abuse, and other forms of child abuse. The public media can cover the subject in social issue programming. In short, only as people become aware of the problem can they prevent it and treat it.

Listen to Children—and Believe Them

"If only my parents had listened to me! If only they'd believed me when I told them what was happening!" Survivors of sibling abuse frequently make these sorts of statements.

In the research mentioned in chapter 5, mothers tended not to believe reports of sexual abuse if they involved a close family member, and if the victim was an older child. For example, mothers were more likely to believe a report of sexual abuse if it involved an uncle but not a husband, and if it was reported by a preschooler instead of a teenager. In the same vein, parents may find it difficult to accept reports of sibling abuse because the abuser is a member of the immediate family. Moreover, if parents have seen some of the abuse, they may decide to ignore it, not to believe that there's a problem, or to blame the victim for it. There's an old saying about not killing the messenger, and, in effect, that is what happens when children report sibling abuse to parents who don't want to deal with it. It is easier to lash out at the messenger—in this case, the victim—than to take steps to stop the abuse.

Research shows that children rarely falsely accuse an adult of sexual abuse. Study after study proves this fact. No false accusations were reported in eighty-eight psychiatric papers published on this topic between 1971 and 1978. In other studies where some children retracted their statements, researchers believe that their families pressured them to do so. Although these studies were on children who reported being abused by adults, their conclusions probably apply to children who report being abused by their siblings.

A Canadian respondent, who was physically, emotionally, and sexually abused by an older brother during most of her childhood, documents parental inaction and disbelief from her own personal experience.

> My parents could have believed me when I told them about the abuse, or they could have tried to stop it. . . . My parents had no reaction but denial.

A man from Connecticut who had been the victim of physical abuse by two older brothers had the same experience.

> I would tell my mother about the way my brothers were treating me, but she always brushed it off. I really don't think she cared what they

did. At least that's the message I got from her. It didn't pay for me to tell her my troubles.

A Kentucky woman who was sexually abused by an older sibling whenever her parents were away from home advises parents to listen to their children.

Please listen to your children, even between the lines. I remember every time my parents went out, I'd sit in their room while they got ready to go out and I'd ask them, "Do you really have to go out tonight? Can't you stay home?"

She was trying to give her parents a message, but they weren't listening.

Parents need to understand what their children feel. If a child cries out because his sibling is always hitting him and calling him names, his parents should empathize—not ask him what he did to provoke it. Parents might complain that empathizing takes too much time and can encourage constant complaining. However, a kind response takes no more time than an unkind one, and parents who empathize are more likely to have children who will tell them what is going on. Children don't usually have anyone but their parents to talk to about serious matters. Unless there is an atmosphere of open communication in the house, they may end up telling no one at all.

In addition to listening and empathizing, parents also need to be sensitive to patterns of behavior in their household. They may realize that the youngest child is always the butt of jokes by an older sibling. They may realize that one child is frequently ridiculed because of being overweight, short, bucktoothed, and so on. In short, they may become aware when their children's rivalry becomes abusive. When parents become aware of these behavior patterns, they can take appropriate steps to break the cycle.

Adele Faber and Elaine Mazlish suggest some excellent ways to help parents really listen to their children in their very practical book *How to Talk So Kids Will Listen and Listen So Kids Will Talk*. This book contains cartoons, parent–child dialogues, and exercises. Parents can use these techniques to analyze the ways they typically talk with their children, and to realize the things that may prevent them from hearing what their children are trying to tell them. These are extremely important skills that are well worth developing. If nothing else, the survivors of sibling abuse have taught us that truth.

An important part of successful, open communication depends on how secrets are handled. Many parents have trouble handling secrets. In most instances, children should be told that they don't need to keep secrets from their parents, no matter who told them to do so—an adult, a brother, or a sister—even if that person has threatened to harm them, their pet, or something they own. Parents should assure children that their secrets will be protected, and that no harm will come to them. This is important, because the secret may be about abuse.

While listening to children, parents and professionals should be alert for signs of physical, emotional, or sexual abuse. The following list of signs may help:

Feelings of worthlessness; low self-image and self-esteem.
Unexplained marks or bruises on the child's body.
Preferring to be alone rather than with siblings or friends.
Living in fantasy.
A sense of sadness or depression; a low energy level or
    withdrawal.
Clinging behavior.
Fear of being left in the care of a sibling.
Sexual self-consciousness or shame about the body.
Lack of knowledge or wrong information about sexual
    behavior.
Repeated and inappropriate sexual play with friends, toys, or
    self.
Shyness, fear, mistrust.
Overly obedient behavior at home or at school.
Sudden changes in school performance.
Nightmares and other sleep problems.
Unexplained fears.
Bed-wetting and other "babyish" behavior for children who are
    older and toilet-trained.
Talking about suicide, or attempting it.
Genital or anal bruising, bleeding, or injury.
Genital itching or pain.
Torn or stained clothing.

Obviously this list doesn't include every sign that children could display. It also doesn't mean that every child who wets his or her bed unexpectedly is being abused by a sibling. Any behavior change, however, may be an important sign that something is bothering a child. That "something" may be sibling abuse.

The people who responded to the questionnaire frequently noted that they couldn't tell their parents about their abuse. Some were afraid they wouldn't be believed; some were afraid they would be blamed. This kind of poor communication can take place when parents are away from home, because of work or other activities. Even when they are at home, parents may be emotionally absent. But all parents, working outside the home or not, can create an atmosphere in which their children feel safe enough to talk about the things that trouble and distress them.

Provide Good Supervision

The number of children who care for themselves after school, or in the evenings, has increased in recent years due to the rising number of women who work full-time. The high divorce rate has meant a large number of single mothers, who are often forced to rely on other people to help with child care. Often, the baby-sitter turns out to be an older sibling. There are no clear, current figures for how many children are taking care of themselves or being cared for by a sibling. However, according to the Current Population Survey in 1984, over 2 million children aged five to thirteen were in this category. Other studies indicate that even more—up to 80 percent of the country's 28.6 million children—are unsupervised by an adult for some period of time. No specific figures are available because parents often don't want community authorities to know that they leave their children alone. From the data that do exist, it is interesting to note that most of these children are not from low-income, single-parent homes that cannot afford child care, but from white, middle-class families living in suburban or rural areas. If the sibling in charge is mature, and if the younger siblings feel comfortable talking with their parents, then this can be a good arrangement. Otherwise, sibling abuse may occur.

Most often, sibling abuse occurs when parents are away and victims are in the care of an older sibling. Survivors repeatedly noted that the sibling in charge couldn't handle this responsibility. A female respondent from Florida wrote:

Parents should wake up and realize that just because a child is the oldest doesn't mean they can take care of the younger children. My folks would always leave us with my older sister. This is when I and my other brothers and sisters suffered. She felt she could do anything she wanted to us. She did.

Sometimes older brothers and sisters do make good baby-sitters, but parents must prepare in advance to make it work well. They should discuss with all their children what they can and cannot do. For example, how long they can watch TV, and which programs they can watch; what they can eat; which appliances they can use; bedtimes; and other important items. They should also check to see how well the sibling in charge handled these responsibilities. In addition, they should discuss these arrangements with all their children, and change them if it seems like they aren't working out.

Concerned parents can also establish latchkey programs for children who come home to empty houses. The United Way can assist in setting up these programs and may even know about safe places—like rooms in office buildings or churches—that can be used to keep children until their parents come home.

One latchkey program that was started by parents is the After School Day Care Association (ASDCA) in Madison, Wisconsin. The organization works closely with public schools but is independent and self-supporting. ASDCA rents nonclassroom space from elementary schools. Recently, it served over seven hundred children every school day, from dismissal to 5:30 P.M. or later. The location of the program is one reason parents like it so much: children can walk from their classrooms directly to the room where the program is held.

Some communities have established telephone support services—like PhoneFriend and KIDLINE—for children who are home alone after school. These services are staffed by volunteers and can handle a wide range of children's problems—like fighting with their brothers and sisters. Although no data exist on how many children discuss sibling abuse with these services, it is one avenue that may provide help.

Community child-care agencies sometimes offer courses on baby-sitting that older siblings may attend before taking on the responsibility of caring for their younger brothers and sisters. This badly needed service, however, is rare. Many parents assume that children can step into their role as substitute parents without much help. Unfortunately, this is a source of a number of problems, including sibling abuse. Parents and professionals need to help organize various types of training and support programs for the latchkey children in their area.

Encourage Openness about Sex

Encouraging openness about sex does not mean parents should wander naked around the house and discuss their sexual preferences. In fact, those sorts of activities might encourage abuse, not prevent it. Encouraging openness means creating a family atmosphere where sexual issues and problems can be discussed without awkwardness.

In an open environment, sexual issues are discussed when appropriate, and children are given sexual information that is understandable for their age and maturity. Body parts and functions are called by their correct names. Doing all this may make some parents feel uncomfortable, but happily there are a lot of excellent books, pamphlets, and videos that can help. These may be available through public libraries, pediatricians, school counselors, and community health departments. Some people believe that sex education makes children interested in sex at very young ages, but there is no research to support this theory. In fact, the opposite is likely to occur. Children who are ignorant, but curious about sex may be more likely to experiment because no one will tell them anything about it. They are more likely to turn to unhealthy sources of sexual information, like pornography, and may be tempted to try things out on a younger sibling.

A friend recently explained how his parents told him "the facts of life" as a young boy. His mother returned home from a shopping trip while he was playing in his room. She yelled up from the kitchen that she had bought him a book. Excited, he ran downstairs to the kitchen to get it. When he got there, his mother told him the book was in a drawer of the living room table. He couldn't understand why his mother would buy him a present and then put it there. When he opened the drawer, he saw that the book was about sex. He remembers thinking that the book was something he should not read when anyone else was around, and that there was something very secret and mysterious about sex. Obviously, this sort of scene does not create an open, positive atmosphere in which children can discuss sex with their parents.

Sex is not something that parents should talk about only once with their children. It is not a single "birds-and-bees" discussion. Sexual information should be given to children at different times in their lives, depending on their age and maturity. For example, younger siblings may need some information about the body changes they are seeing in their older siblings who are going through puberty.

An open and positive attitude about sex also means that children have a right to privacy, or times and places where they can be alone. While children may have to share a bedroom, their furniture can be arranged in such a way as to give them some space of their own. Parents must also set rules about privacy in the bathroom.

Being candid about sex also means that parents must respond when their children see films or TV programs that show sex in a degrading way, and when their children make sexual remarks, jokes, or suggestions to one another. The victims of sexual abuse found that their parents ignored sexually slanted remarks, and this helped create the problem. Perhaps because their parents let unhealthy aspects of sex exist in the home, their siblings thought that sexual abuse would be tolerated. This seems especially true for older boys who sexually abuse their younger sisters.

Let Children Own Their Own Bodies

Children have a right to own their own bodies. If this seems like an obvious statement, it's not. They have a right to be hugged and kissed and touched only when they want to be, and only by the people they want to have hug, kiss, and touch them. Equally, they have a right to say no to the people they don't want near them—for whatever reason. However, parents must make a conscious effort to let children own their own bodies. This involves a process of education.

In recent years, a number of programs have been developed to help children protect themselves from becoming sexual victims. They focus a great deal on how to say no to touches and approaches that can lead to sexual abuse. Children are taught, for example, what is a good touch and what is a bad or secret touch. Good touches are the normal hugs, kisses, and roughhousing that both parents and children may want to do. Bad touches are sexual, or in places that are private, like breasts and genitals. Bad touches may also include tickling when a child wants it to stop. In short, children must be taught that their bodies are their own property, and under their own control.

Programs to prevent physical abuse usually focus on teaching the abuser to work out problems without violence. Programs to prevent sexual abuse are aimed at teaching potential victims how to resist being abused. This difference in approach is due to the fact that most sex abusers don't think they need help. Also, victims of sex abuse are often older than victims of physical abuse, so they can be taught more easily. Finally, sex abuse often happens because children don't know enough about sex and may be tricked into it. If they knew what it was, they could recognize and refuse it.

While many films, videos, cartoon strips, coloring books, and other items are available to teach children about sex abuse, they are usually geared to abuse by adults. However, they can be adapted to include sexual abuse by siblings. For information on programs to prevent sex abuse that have been used in schools, churches, scout troops, and similar organizations, contact the National Committee for the Prevention of Child Abuse (NCPCA), 332 South Michigan Boulevard, Suite 1600, Chicago, Illinois 60604-4357; or call them at 312/663-3520. This is a nationwide network of agencies dedicated to preventing the physical, emotional, and sexual abuse of children and has chapters in all fifty states. The NCPCA will give the name, address, and phone number of the nearest state chapter office which can provide helpful information on preventing abuse of all kinds.

A list of audiovisual materials that can be used in designing a program to prevent sexual abuse can be found in a book edited by P.B. Mrazek and C.H. Kempe, called *Sexually Abused Children and Their Families*. The section by G. Deitrich contains a list of materials and a review of each one.

The Committee on Children publishes a free catalog of training materials, including videos and books, recommended to prevent child abuse and violence. Its VHS video for children in grades 2 to

6, called *Yes, You Can Say No,* has received nine major awards, including an Emmy. It focuses on a ten-year-old boy who is sexually abused by a once-trusted adult, and who learns how to say no and regain control of the situation. For more information, contact The Committee on Children, at 172 20th Avenue, Seattle, Washington 98122; or call 206/322-5050.

There are excellent pamphlets and books that can be used to teach children how to avoid sexual abuse. They are available at the public library, bookstores, or through the state or national NCPCA office.

Efforts to prevent child sexual abuse must begin early in a child's life. Yet one study conducted in Boston found that less than a third of 521 parents of children aged six to fourteen had talked to their children about sex abuse. Only a fifth of those who did discuss sexual abuse mentioned that it could come from a family member. Most parents believed that children should be about nine years old before they learn about sex and sex abuse. For many of the survivors of sexual abuse in this book, nine would have been much too late. They were already victims many times over by then. Most parents just didn't look at their children as potential victims and assumed that the abusers would be strangers, not family members and friends.

Many parents don't like talking to children about sex abuse because they don't want to frighten them. But parents educate their children about many other dangers, such as animals, stoves, cars, and matches, without scaring them. Other parents are afraid to discuss abuse because they believe it will make their children frightened of adults.

Research, however, proves that knowledge—not ignorance— helps children defend themselves.

Seeking Help for Sibling Abuse

If parents notice an abusive pattern of behavior among their children, they may need professional help to stop it. For example, an older brother is constantly making fun of his little sister and upsetting her. Although his parents ask him to stop, he continues to think up new and different ways to irritate her.

Often, parents don't want to admit that they need professional help. It seems like a sign of weakness or defeat. However, abuse does not usually end without certain changes being made, and not all parents know how to make them. Although most adults cheerfully turn to experts to tune their car engines, clean their teeth, and fix the plumbing or electrical wiring in their houses, they often don't want to take their children to mental health workers. For some reason, many people believe they should have been born knowing how to parent and how to tackle any child-related problem that crops up. Life simply doesn't work that way.

Another reason why parents may not like to take children to therapists is because they are afraid of being blamed for the problem. Recent research, however, shows that genetics often determines how children turn out, not their parents' behavior.

Thus, two children from the same family may be completely different individuals. The first child may be easygoing, sweet-natured, and gentle-spirited from the day he or she was born. The second child, however, may be unruly, constantly testing, and aggressive. Even though their parents treat them the same way, the children act in opposite ways. If parents find themselves saying, "That kid sure has a mind of his own," they're right. Children do have their own temperaments and preferences, and parents may need to treat them differently from their siblings.

Where should parents go for help? If they don't know of anyone personally, or through their friends, a quick glance through the Yellow Pages can help. Under the heading of "Marriage and Family Counselors," parents should find a number of options. Some community services have fees based on what each family can afford. Agencies generally don't charge as much as private therapists. Families who prefer to use private therapists should check their health insurance policies, as counseling is sometimes covered.

Families should check the credentials of private therapists. Some states require counselors to be licensed, and that can be checked through state medical licensing organizations. Families may also ask if therapists are members of professional organizations like the American Association of Marriage and Family Therapists (AAMFT), the American Psychological Association (APA), or the National Association of Social Workers (NASW). Family counseling agencies may be a part of the Family Services Association of America (FSAA), an association where members must meet certain professional standards.

A final note: Families should not seek professional help for children with the idea that they are going to be "fixed." Although the children may be the focus of the counseling, they are only expressing problems that affect the whole family. Parents and siblings can expect to get involved in whole-family therapy so that counselors can see where the problems are and suggest how to work on them. In families where sibling abuse is a problem, therapists report that effective treatment must include the whole family, not just the victim and the abuser.

Seeking professional help is a sign of strength, not weakness. Parents are telling their children that they love them when they say, "We know you are not happy. We are concerned. We love you and we want to do something about this. Let's get some help as a family."

Violence-Proof the Home

We live in a violent society. Turn on the TV, read a newspaper, or check out the movies, and it appears we thrive on violence. Obviously, society is not going to become less violent any time soon. However, each of us can make a contribution toward a safer, more peaceful existence in our own lives and in the lives of people we touch. Families can violence-proof their homes and, in a sense, themselves.

This can be done in several ways. First, it is important to be aware of the violence that comes into the home through TV. Parents should screen the programs their children watch. Violence creates more violence; it spreads and reproduces itself. It can prompt violence within the family. As one victim of sibling abuse put it:

> Kids mirror what they see, whether it be on TV, in the movies, or in what they may even read. If as adults we aren't alert to what kids are being exposed to, how can we expect them to behave any differently from the "Rambo images" they are watching?

Screening out the violence that children watch on television and in films helps reduce its impact on them.

Another important way adults can help reduce violence in the home is to be aware of how their children treat one another. Nasty comments often come before other, more physical abuse like slapping and hitting. Comments that are sexual in nature may be a warning of upcoming sex abuse. Parents and other adults have a responsibility to help children feel good about themselves and to encourage kindness to others. Parents also should make sure their own relationships are in order, because children often mimic what they see.

Pushing, shoving, hitting, and other acts of violence should not be ignored. Children must be given the message that physical abuse is not acceptable. However, screaming and hitting children who have just screamed and hit their siblings is not the way to teach peace and harmony in the household. Taking them aside privately and explaining why abusive behavior is not allowed can be a good experience for children. Otherwise, they may assume that hitting, ridiculing, and similar actions are appropriate with friends and siblings.

Reward Good Behavior

Children often live in a world of "don't." Adults, especially parents, who take care of children can use the word a great deal. "Don't hit your sister." "Don't make a mess." "Don't call your brother names." "Don't bring your dirty shoes into the house." Because these behaviors are quickly noticed, parents quickly respond to them. However, children who behave well may not be congratulated nearly as often as they are scolded when they behave badly.

When children act in positive ways, they should be told that, too. Parents may say, "I noticed how well you played with your little sister today. I'm really proud of you." Teachers might say, "It's wonderful to see how well you and your sister get along." Positive actions that are noticed and praised encourage children to continue them. It also makes them feel good about themselves, which helps develop their self-esteem. When children are rewarded for their positive behavior, they enjoy the good feelings they get and are less likely to become abusive.

Preventing sibling abuse follows naturally on the heels of understanding. Once parents become aware and understand the importance of good communication and supervision, the serious consequences of this form of abuse can be averted.

A Final Word

The statistics are devastating. The words of the survivors are horrifying. And yet, sibling abuse continues unchecked in our society.
The 150 people who answered the questionnaire that forms the
basis for this book are, in a sense, the lucky ones—the survivors—
who are in counseling and receiving help. They probably represent
a tiny fraction of those who were abused by siblings. Most survivors
probably have not gotten therapy and must live with the effects of
sibling abuse every day. For the writers of this book, there is a kind
of death knell that accompanies the figures below:

Eighty-nine percent, or 134 of the respondents, were female; 11
   percent, or 16 of them, were male.
Respondents ranged in age from eighteen to seventy-seven, with
   an average age of thirty-seven.
Eighty-five percent, or 127 people who responded, were white,
   the rest were mostly black or of other ethnic backgrounds.
Twenty-seven percent, or 40 of the respondents, were single.
   Forty-seven percent, or 71 of them, were married. Three
   percent, or 4 of them, were living with someone but not
   married. Twenty-one percent, or 31, were divorced. Only one
   person was widowed.
The respondents were well-educated. Only 16 percent, or 24,
   had a high school education or less. Fifty percent, or 75 of
   them, had attended college or completed it. Another 34
   percent, or 51 people, had completed graduate school.
The educational level of survivors' parents was also examined.
   Fifty-seven percent, or 85 of the respondents, had mothers
   with a high school education or less. Forty-three percent, or
   65, had mothers who had attended college, completed

college, or had a graduate degree. Almost the same number of respondents' fathers had the same levels of education. Only one more father had attended or completed college.

As much as possible, it was determined that survivors' families had middle-class incomes.

Sixty-three percent, or 94 of the survivors, thought their mothers were religious; 37 percent, or 56 of them, did not. Only 40 percent, or 59 of them, thought their fathers were religious; 60 percent, or 91 respondents, did not. Thirty-three percent, or 50 of the respondents, thought their mothers' religious beliefs played a strong role in their upbringing; 20 percent, or 35, thought their fathers' religious beliefs were very influential.

Families of survivors had anywhere from two to thirteen children. The average family size was three children. Thus, most respondents had more than one sibling. It was not too important whether the victims were the middle or youngest children; but in 90 percent, or 135 of the cases in this book, the abusive sibling was the oldest child. In most cases the abusive sibling was male, although in 27 percent, or 46 of the cases, sisters joined brothers in being abusive.

In many cases, it seems that the abuse was concentrated on one child. However, survivors may not have been aware of the abuse suffered by other siblings, especially sexual abuse.

Twenty-eight percent, or 42 of the respondents, thought their fathers were abusing their mothers. In these cases, abusive siblings may have been practicing what they saw at home.

Forty-five percent, or 68 of the victims of sexual abuse, shared a bedroom with a sibling; 55 percent, or 82, did not.

Almost 25 percent, or 39 respondents, had been hospitalized for depression. It may be assumed that an even higher number were treated for depression outside of a hospital setting.

Twenty-eight percent, or 42 of the survivors in this book, had problems with abuse of drugs, alcohol, or food; 72 percent, or 108 of them, did not.

One third, or 50 of the respondents, had attempted suicide at least once. As mentioned earlier, experts at the American Association of Suicidology believe that less than one percent of the general population ever attempts suicide.

The Abusers

There are no statistics, no information, no quotes from the abusers. They remain silent and protected. Questions about them remain unanswered. Who are they? Are they this generation's wife-beaters or child-molesters? Have they gone to prison for other violent crimes? Or, are they upstanding, respected members of our society—teachers, college presidents, business leaders, store owners, members of Congress? One question that begs to be answered about the abusers is whether or not they feel any guilt. Do they even recognize what they have done to the children they call brother and sister? Research on how to prevent and treat sibling abuse, and laws that will stop it, are desperately needed. If children are legally protected from their parents, and spouses are protected from one another, shouldn't children be protected from the siblings who abuse them?

Conclusion

Some people will read this book because of the title. They may have seen themselves in it. Some may have been abused as children—not by their parents or other adults, but by their siblings. They may strongly identify with the survivors in this book. It is important for these readers to know that help is available. They are not fated for a life of emotional pain and suffering. However, they should seek help for the effects of their past. They also can be extremely helpful in working with abused children, because they understand their pain.

Other readers will be luckier. They will not have been abused as children. But they also may wish to help others who have been abused. There are a lot of ways to do this—as volunteers with local agencies working in family violence, at battered spouse shelters, at day-care centers for abused children, and in support groups for abused members. Contact a community social agency to find out how to help. This could mark the beginning of bringing sibling abuse and personal violence to an end in this society.

Bibliography

The following books and articles were used in the research for this book on sibling abuse. Individuals interested in learning more about the studies and findings cited, or in reading the books mentioned in the text, will find them referenced here by chapter.

Chapter 1

J. Demos, *Past, Present and Personal* (New York: Oxford University Press, 1986), 69.

D. Russell, *Secret Trauma* (New York: Basic Books, 1986).

Chapter 2

M. Strauss, R. Gelles, and S. Steinmetz, *Behind Closed Doors* (Garden City, N.Y.: Anchor Books, 1980).

S. Steinmetz, *The Cycle of Violence: Assertive, Aggressive and Abusive Family Interaction* (New York: Praeger, 1977).

"Battered families: A growing nightmare," *U.S. News & World Report,* 15 January 1979, 60–61.

L. Farrell, "The touching truth about tickling," *Mademoiselle,* April 1985, 54, 56.

A. Freud, *The Ego and the Mechanisms of Defense* (London: Hogarth Press, 1946), 117.

Chapter 3

S. Hart and M. Brassard, "A major threat to children's mental health—Psychological maltreatment," *American Psychologist* 42 (1987): 160–65.

S. Hart, R. Germain, and M. Brassard, "The challenge: To better understand and combat the psychological maltreatment of children and youth," in *Psychological Maltreatment of Children and Youth,* eds. M. Brassard, R. Germain, and S. Hart (New York: Pergamon Press, 1987); I. Lourie and L. Stefano, "On defining emotional abuse," in *Child Abuse and Neglect: Issues in Innovation and Implementation: Proceedings of the Second Annual National Conference on Child Abuse and Neglect,* eds. M. Lauderdale, R. Anderson, and S. Cramer (Washington, D.C.: U.S. Government Printing Office, 1978): DHEW [DHDS] 78-30147, vol. 1, 201–208.

J. Garbarino and J. Vondra, "Psychological maltreatment: Issues and perspectives," in Brassard, Germain, and Hart, *Psychological Maltreatment;* Hart, Germain, and Brassard, "The challenge."

M. Brassard and M. Gelardo, "Psychological maltreatment: The unifying construct in child abuse and neglect," *School Psychology Review* 16 (1987): 127–36.

J. Corson and H. Davidson, "Emotional abuse and the law," in Brassard, Germain, and Hart, *Psychological Maltreatment;* E. Navarre, "Psychological maltreatment: The core component of child abuse," in Brassard, Germain, and Hart, *Psychological Maltreatment.*

J. Garbarino, E. Guttmann, and J. Seeley, *The Psychologically Battered Child* (San Francisco: Jossey-Bass, 1986).

E. Berne, *Games People Play* (New York: Grove Press, 1967).

D. Kline, *The Disabled Child and Child Abuse* (Chicago: National Committee for the Prevention of Child Abuse, 1982).

Apocrypha to the Bible (King James Version). Ecclesiasticus (Sirach) 28:16–18.

Chapter 4

D. Finkelhor and L. Baron, "Risk factors for child sexual abuse," *Journal of Interpersonal Violence* 1 (1986): 43–71.

J. O'Brien, *Characteristics of Male Adolescent Sibling Incest Offenders* (Orwell, Vt.: The Safer Society Program, 1989).

D. Walters, *Physical and Sexual Abuse of Children: Causes and Treatment* (Bloomington, Ind.: Indiana University Press, 1975).

P. Gebhard, J. Gagnon, W. Pomeroy, and C. Christenson, *Sex Offenders: An Analysis of Types* (New York: Harper and Row, 1965).

D. Finkelhor, *Child Sexual Abuse: New Theory and Research* (New York: Free Press, 1984).

D. Finkelhor, "Sex among siblings: A survey of prevalence, variety, and effects," *Archives of Sexual Behavior* 9 (1980): 171–93.

D. Russell, *Secret Trauma* (New York: Basic Books, 1986).

L. Muldoon, ed., *Incest: Confronting the Silent Crime* (St. Paul, Minn.: Minnesota Program for Victims of Sexual Assault, 1979); D. Russell, *Rape in Marriage* (New York: Macmillan, 1982).

J. Goodwin, *Sexual Abuse: Incest Victims and Their Families* (Boston: John W. Wright, 1982).

K. Faller, "Characteristics of a clinical sample of sexually abused children: How boy and girl victims differ," *Child Abuse and Neglect* 13 (1989): 281–91.

J. Benward and J. Densen-Gerber, "Incest as a causative factor in antisocial behavior: An explanatory study," *Contemporary Drug Problems* 4 (1975): 323–40.

J. Herman and L. Hirschman, "Father-daughter incest," *Signs: Journal of Women in Culture and Society* 4 (1977): 735–56.

E. Bliss, *Multiple Personality, Allied Disorders and Hypnosis* (New York: Oxford University Press, 1986).

W. Confer and B. Ables, *Multiple Personality* (New York: Human Sciences Press, 1983); C. Wilbur, "Multiple personality and child abuse: An overview," *Psychiatric Clinics of North America* 7 (1984): 3–7.

R. Summit, "Child sexual abuse accommodation syndrome," *Child Abuse and Neglect* 7 (1983): 177–93.

A. Burgess and L. Holmstrom, "Sexual trauma of children and adolescents: Pressure, sex, secrecy," *Nursing Clinics of North America* 10 (1975): 551–63.

Chapter 5

R. Felson and N. Russo, "Parental punishment and sibling aggression," *Social Psychology Quarterly* 51 (1988): 11–18.

E. Sirles and P. Franke, "Factors influencing mothers' reactions to intrafamily sexual abuse," *Child Abuse and Neglect* 13 (1989): 131–39.

J. Benward and J. Densen-Gerber, "Incest as a causative factor in antisocial behavior: An explanatory study," *Contemporary Drug Problems* 4 (1975): 323–40.

S. Sgroi, *Vulnerable Populations: Evaluation and Treatment of Sexually Abused Children and Adult Survivors,* vol. 1 (Lexington, Mass.: Lexington Books, 1988).

N. Brill, *Working with People* (New York: Longman, 1985).

Chapter 6

H. Blalock, *Causal Inferences in Nonexperimental Research* (Chapel Hill: University of North Carolina Press, 1964).

S. Peele, *The Diseasing of America* (Lexington, Mass.: Lexington Books, 1989).

R. Galdston, "Observations on children who have been physically abused and their parents," *American Journal of Psychiatry* 122 (1965): 440–43.

B. Steele and C. Pollock, "A psychiatric study of parents who abuse infants and small children," in *The Battered Child,* eds. R. Helfer and C. Kempe (Chicago: University of Chicago Press, 1968); H. Martin, "The environment of the abused child," in *The Abused Child: A Multidisciplinary Approach to Developmental Issues and Treatment,* ed. H. Martin (Cambridge: Ballinger, 1976).

H. Smith and E. Israel, "Sibling incest: A study of the dynamics of 25 cases," *Child Abuse and Neglect* 11 (1987): 101–108.

J. Garbarino, "The human ecology of child maltreatment: A conceptual model for research," *Journal of Marriage and the Family* 39 (1977): 721–35; R. Parke and C. Collmer, "Child abuse: An interdisciplinary analysis," in *Child Development Research,* ed. E. Hetherington (Chicago: University of Chicago Press, 1975); V.

Wiehe, "Child abuse: An ecological perspective," in *Child Abuse and Neglect: Theory, Research and Practice,* ed. R. Pardeck (New York: Gordon and Breach, 1989).

J. Belsky, "Child maltreatment: An ecological integration," *American Psychologist* 35 (1980): 320–35.

D. Bakan, *Slaughter of the Innocents* (San Francisco: Jossey-Bass, 1971).

K. Magid and C. McKelvey, *High Risk* (New York: Bantam, 1987).

D. Glaser, "Violence in the society," in *Violence in the Home: Interdisciplinary Perspectives,* ed. M. Lystad (New York: Brunner/Mazel, 1986).

A. Faber and E. Mazlish, *Siblings without Rivalry* (New York: Avon Books, 1987).

L. Berkowitz, "The case for bottling up rage," *Psychology Today* 7 (1973): 24–31.

S. Feshbach, "The function of aggression and the regulation of aggressive drive," *Psychological Review* 71 (1964): 257–72.

M. Strauss, R. Gelles, and S. Steinmetz, *Behind Closed Doors* (Garden City, N.Y.: Anchor Books, 1980).

C. Tavris, *Anger: The Misunderstood Emotion* (New York: Simon and Schuster, 1982).

C. Zastrow and K. Kirst-Ashman, *Understanding Human Behavior and the Social Environment* (Chicago: Nelson-Hall, 1987).

A. Bellak, "Comparable worth: A practitioner's view," in *Comparable Worth: Issue for the 80's, A Consultation for the U.S. Commission on Civil Rights* (June 6–7, 1982): 75–82.

D. Davidson, *Conjugal Crime: Understanding and Changing the Wife-Beating Pattern* (New York: Hawthorne, 1978); R. E. Dobash and R. P. Dobash, *Violence against Wives* (New York: Free Press, 1981); L. Walker, *The Battered Woman Syndrome* (New York: Spring, 1984).

D. Russell, *Secret Trauma* (New York: Basic Books, 1986).

S. Brownmiller, *Against Our Will* (New York: Bantam Books, 1975).

Chapter 7

J. Garbarino, E. Guttmann, and J. Seeley, *The Psychologically Battered Child* (San Francisco: Jossey-Bass, 1986).

K. Faller, "Characteristics of a clinical sample of sexually abused children: How boy and girl victims differ," *Child Abuse and Neglect* 13 (1989): 281–91; J. Herman and L. Hirschman, "Father-daughter incest," *Signs: Journal of Women in Culture and Society* 4 (1977): 735–56; L. McGuire and N. Wagner, "Sexual dysfunction in women who were molested as children: One response pattern and suggestions for treatment," *Journal of Sex and Marital Therapy* 1 (1978): 11–15; R. Summit and J. Kryso, "Sexual abuse of children: A clinical spectrum," *Clinical Social Work Journal* 1 (1978): 62–77.

L. Walker, *The Battered Woman Syndrome* (New York: Spring, 1984).

C. Agosta and M. Loring, "Understanding and treating the adult retrospective victim of child sexual abuse," in *Vulnerable Populations,* ed. S. Sgroi, vol. 1 (Lexington, Mass.: Lexington Books, 1988): 119–20.

C. Black, *"It Will Never Happen to Me!"* (New York: Ballantine Books, 1981).

J. Blake-White and M. Kline, "Treating the dissociative process in adult victims of childhood incest," *Social Casework* 66 (1985): 394–402.

H. Lerner, *The Dance of Anger* (New York: Harper and Row, 1985): 10.

J. Hollis, *Fat Is a Family Affair* (New York: Harper/Hazelden, 1985).

D. Gelinas, "The persisting negative effects of incest," *Psychiatry* 46 (1983): 312–32.

D. Finkelhor, *Child Sexual Abuse: New Theory and Research* (New York: Free Press, 1984).

J. Briere, "The effects of childhood sexual abuse on later psychological functioning: Defining a post-sexual abuse syndrome." Paper presented at the Third National Conference on Sexual Victimization of Children, Children's Hospital National Medical Center, Washington, D.C. (April 1984); K. Meiselman, *Incest: A Psychological Study of Causes and Effects with Treatment Recommendations* (San Francisco: Jossey-Bass, 1978).

E. Blume, "The walking wounded: Post-incest syndrome," *SIECUS Report XV* 1 (September 1986): 5–7; M. Janus, "On early sexual victimization and adolescent male prostitution," *SIECUS Report XII* 1 (September 1984): 8–9; M. Silbert and A. Pines, "Early sexual exploitation as an influence in prostitution," *Social Work* 2 (1983): 285–89.

J. Benward and J. Densen-Gerber, "Incest as a causative factor in antisocial behavior: An explanatory study," *Contemporary Drug Problems* 4 (1975): 323–40.

F. Cohen and J. Densen-Gerber, "A study of the relationship between child abuse and drug addiction in 178 patients: Preliminary results," *Child Abuse and Neglect* 6 (1982): 383–87; D. Rohsenow, R. Corbett, and D. Devine, "Molested as children: A hidden contribution to substance abuse?" *Journal of Substance Abuse Treatment* 5 (1988): 13–18.

M. Johanek, "Treatment of male victims of child sexual abuse in military service," in *Vulnerable Populations,* ed. S. Sgroi, vol. 1 (Lexington, Mass.: Lexington Books, 1988).

G. Edwall and N. Hoffman, "Correlates of incest reported by adolescent girls in treatment for substance abuse," in *Handbook on Sexual Abuse of Children,* ed. L. Auberbach Walker (New York: Springer, 1988).

M. Singer, M. Petchers, and D. Hussey, "The relationship between sexual abuse and substance abuse among psychiatrically hospitalized adolescents," *Child Abuse and Neglect* 13 (1989): 319–25.

C. Bagley and R. Ramsey, "Disrupted childhood and vulnerability to sexual assault: Long-term sequels with implications for counseling." Paper presented at the Conference on Counseling the Sexual Abuse Survivor, Winnepeg, Canada (February 1985); S. Peters, "The relationship between childhood sexual victimization and adult depression among Afro-American and white women." Unpublished Ph.D. diss., University of California, Los Angeles (1984); M. Sedney and B. Brooks, "Factors associated with a history of childhood sexual experience in a non-clinical female population," *Journal of the American Academy of Child Psychiatry* 23 (1984): 215–18.

J. Briere and M. Runtz, "Symptomatology associated with prior sexual abuse in a non-clinical sample," *Child Abuse and Neglect* 12 (1988): 51–59.

M. DeYoung, *The Sexual Victimization of Children* (Jefferson, N.C.: McFarland, 1982).

J. Briere, D. Evans, M. Runtz, and T. Wall, "Symptomatology in men who were molested as children: A comparison study," *American Journal of Orthopsychiatry* 58 (1988): 457–61.

Diagnostic and Statistical Manual of Mental Disorders, 3rd ed. (Washington, D.C.: American Psychiatric Association, 1987), 247.

S. Patten, Y. Gatz, B. Jones, and D. Thomas, "Posttraumatic stress disorder and the treatment of sexual abuse," *Social Work* 34 (1989): 197–203.

A. Rosenfeld, "Incidence of a history of incest among 18 female psychiatric patients," *American Journal of Psychiatry* 136 (1979): 791–95.

Chapter 8

A. Faber and E. Mazlish, *Siblings without Rivalry* (New York: Avon Books, 1987); A. Faber and E. Mazlish, *How to Talk So Kids Will Listen and Listen So Kids Will Talk* (New York: Avon Books, 1980).

J. Vander Zanden, *Human Development* (New York: Knopf, 1985).

A. Burgess and L. Holmstrom, "Sexual trauma of children and adolescents: Pressure, sex, secrecy," *Nursing Clinics of North America* 10 (1975): 551–63; R. Summit, "Child sexual abuse accommodation syndrome," *Child Abuse and Neglect* 7 (1983): 177–93.

Chapter 9

E. Sirles and P. Franke, "Factors influencing mothers' reactions to intrafamily sexual abuse," *Child Abuse and Neglect* 13 (1989): 131–39.

H. Cantwell, "Sexual abuse of children in Denver, 1979: Reviewed with implications for pediatric intervention and possible prevention," *Child Abuse and Neglect* 5 (1981): 75–85.

J. Goodwin, D. Sahd, and R. Rada, "False accusations and false denials of incest: Clinical myths and clinical realities," in *Sexual Abuse: Incest Victims and Their Families,* ed. J. Goodwin (Boston: John W. Wright, 1982).

J. Peters, "Children who are victims of sexual assault and the psychology of offenders," *American Journal of Psychotherapy* 30 (1976): 398–421.

T. Reik, *Listening with the Third Ear* (New York: Grove Press, 1948).

A. Faber and E. Mazlish, *How to Talk So Kids Will Listen and Listen So Kids Will Talk* (New York: Avon Books, 1980).

R. Bruno, "After-school care of school-age children: December 1984," *Current Population Reports,* series P-23, no. 149 (Washington, D.C.: U.S. Government Printing Office, 1987).

L. Steinberg, "Latchkey children and susceptibility to peer pressure: An ecological analysis," *Childhood Education* 22 (1986): 433–39.

V. Cain and S. Hofferth, "Parental choice of self-care for school-age children," *Journal of Marriage and the Family* 51 (1989): 65–77.

L. Guerney and L. Moore, "PhoneFriend: A prevention-oriented service for latchkey children," *Children Today* 12 (1978): 5–10; A. Nichols and R. Schilit, "Telephone support for latchkey children," *Child Welfare* 67 (1988): 49–59.

D. Finkelhor, *Child Sexual Abuse: New Theory and Research* (New York: Free Press, 1984).

G. Deitrich, "Audiovisual materials with critique," in *Sexually Abused Children and Their Families,* eds. P. Mrazek and H. Kempe (Oxford: Pergamon Press, 1981).

L. Sanford, *The Silent Children: A Parent's Guide to the Prevention of Child Sexual Abuse* (New York: McGraw-Hill, 1982).

J. Conte, R. Rosen, L. Saperstein, and R. Shermack, "An evaluation of a program to prevent sexual victimization of young children," *Child Abuse and Neglect* 9 (1985): 319–28.

G. Patterson, *Coercive Family Process* (Eugene, Ore.: Castalia Publishing Company, 1982); A. Thomas and S. Chess, *Temperament and Development* (New York: Brunner/Mazel, 1977).

J. Bodmer-Turner and E. Kaplan, "A model for treatment of sibling incest." Paper presented at the National Symposium on Child Abuse, Anaheim, Calif. (April 1988).

Chapter 10

D. Finkelhor, *Child Sexual Abuse: New Theory and Research* (New York: Free Press, 1984).

D. Royse, *Research Methods for Social Workers* (Chicago: Nelson-Hall, 1990).

R. Bogdan and S. Taylor, *Introduction to Qualitative Research Methods* (New York: John Wiley and Sons, 1975).

R. Parke and C. Collmer, "Child abuse: An interdisciplinary analysis," in *Child Development Research,* ed. E. Hetherington (Chicago: University of Chicago Press, 1975).

Index

Accessory-to-sex victims, 63
After School Day Care Association, 131
Alcoholism, 87, 140
American Association of Marriage and Family Therapists, 136
American Psychological Association, 136
Anger, abuse as, 92–94
Awareness of sibling abuse, 125–126

Battered child syndrome, 4
BB guns, 13–14
Believing children's reports of abuse, 75–76
Blaming the victim, 72–74

Causes of sibling abuse. *See* Understanding
Choking, 15–16
Committee for Children, 134
Counseling, 135–137
Criteria for distinguishing abuse from normal behavior, 116–124; age appropriateness of behavior, 118–120; how often and how long behavior has occurred, 120–121; purpose of behavior, 122–123; supplementary questions, 123–124; victimization, 121–122

Degrading the victim, 30–36
Deitrich, G., 134
Demos, J., 4
Depression, 112–113, 140
Drowning, 16
Drug abuse, 111–112, 140

Eating disorders, 111–112
Education, of research participants, 139; of research participants' parents, 139
Effects of sibling abuse on victim, 96–115; anger toward perpetrator, 107–109; continued self-blame, 106–107; depression, 112–113, 140; difficulty with interpersonal relationships, 101–104; eating disorders, alcoholism, and drug abuse, 111–112; flashbacks, 113–114; low self-esteem, 96–98; overly sensitive, 105–106; positive effects, 114–115; problems in relationships with opposite sex, 98–101; repeated victimization, 104–105; sexual problems, 109–111
Emotional abuse, 24–44 definition of, 25–26; degrading the victim, 30–36; destroying possessions, 37–39; promoting fear, 36–37; identifying, 25; incidence of, 25–27; name calling, 27–28; ridicule, 29–30; torture or destruction of a pet, 39–40; survivors' response, 40–42

Faber, A., 92, 120, 128
Family Services Association of America, 136
Feigning sleep to avoid sexual abuse, 62–63
Flashbacks, 113–114
Freud, A., 21

Good touches and secret touches, 133–135

Handicapped, abuse of, 37

Identification with the aggressor, 21
Ignoring sibling abuse, 69–72
Inappropriate expectations, 85–86
Inappropriate expression of anger, 92–94
Incest. *See* Sexual abuse
Injurious physical abuse, 12–16
Intergenerational theory of abuse, 90

Kempe, C., 4, 134
KIDLINE, 131

Latch-key programs, 131
Life-threatening abuse, 12–16; choking, 15–16; drowning, 16; shot with BB gun, 13–14; smothering, 15–16
"Lording it" over sibling, 34

Mazlish, 92, 120, 128
Mrazek, P., 134
Multiple personality, 62

Name calling, 27–28
National Association of Social Workers, 136
National Committee for Prevention of Child Abuse, 134

Open communication with children, 127–130, 132–133

Parental awareness of sibling abuse, 67–68
Parental reactions to sibling abuse, 67–83; blaming the victim, 72–74; disbelieving, 75–76; effective and appropriate response, 80–83; ignoring or minimizing abuse, 69–72; inappropriate response, 77–79; indifference, 76; joining in the abuse, 79–80
PhoneFriend, 131
Physical abuse, 7–23; definition, 7; incidence of, 8; injurious or life-threatening, 12–16; most common forms, 8–11; tickling, 11–12; victim's response, 18–22
Post-traumatic stress disorder (PTSD), 113–114

Power, abuse of, 17–18
Preventing sibling abuse, 125–138; build awareness, 125–126; encourage openness about sex, 132–133; give permission to own bodies, 133–135; listen to and believe children, 127–130; provide good supervision, 130–132; reward good behavior, 138; seek help, 135–137; violence-proof home, 137–138
Problem-solving approach, 80–83
Psychological maltreatment. *See* Emotional abuse
Punishment, 77–79

Rape, definition of, 56–57
Research on sibling abuse, brief description 5; data collection, 4–5; description of respondents, 139–140; questionnaire, 5
Reasons for sibling abuse. *See* Understanding
Rewarding good sibling interactions, 138
Ridicule, 29–30

SAFE, 80–83
Self-blame for sexual abuse, 106–107
Sexual abuse, 45–66; baby-sitting, 53–56; blaming the victim, 50–51; definition, 45; disbelieving victim, 75–76; earliest memories, 48–51; escalation, 57; frequency, 46–47; interaction with physical and emotional abuse, 47; parental belief of, 76; trickery, 51–52; victims' response, 62–64; vulnerable age, 46–47; what usually happens, 56–62
Sexual abuse accommodation syndrome, 64–65
Sexual curiosity, 65–66
Sexual dysfunctioning, effect of sexual abuse, 109–111
Smothering, 15–16
Socialization of males, 94–95
Substance abuse, 87–88, 111–112, 140
Suicide, 140
Summit, R., 64
Supervision of children in parents' absence, 130–132

Tavris, C., 94
Teasing, 25, 27
Tickling, 11–12
Trickery, 51–52

Understanding sibling abuse, 84–95;
   behavior viewed as normal, 91–92;
   contribution of victim, 88–89;
   inappropriate expectations, 85–86;
   inappropriate expression of anger,
   92–94; ineffective interventions,

89–91; parents overwhelmed by
   own problems, 87–88; socialization
   of males, 94–95
United Way, 131
U.S. News & World Report, 8

Violence-proof home, 137–138
Victim, repeating victim role,
   104–105

Withdrawn behavior, 63–64

About the Authors

Vernon R. Wiehe is a professor in the College of Social Work at the University of Kentucky at Lexington. After he received a master's degree from the University of Chicago, he did postgraduate work in the Program of Advanced Studies in Social Work at Smith College and studied in Europe. He received his Ph.D. from Washington University in St. Louis. The research reported in his recent book, *Sibling Abuse: Hidden Physical, Emotional, and Sexual Trauma,* published by Lexington Books, was the basis for this book. His numerous publications in professional journals focus on social services to children and families. He has lectured extensively on the subject of domestic violence in the United States and abroad.

Teresa S. Herring is a professional freelance writer who specializes in social issues. Under another name, she has written several books, including *How to Keep Control of Your Life after 50: A Guide for Your Legal, Medical, and Financial Well-Being,* and *Caring for an Aging World* and coauthored *Losing a Million Minds: Confronting the Tragedy of Alzheimer's Disease and Other Dementias;* she has also written numerous articles on science, medicine, and society. Ms. Herring currently resides in Maryland.